THE GARDENS OF
ELLEN BIDDLE SHIPMAN

THE LIBRARY of

AMERICAN
LANDSCAPE
HISTORY

THE GARDENS OF ELLEN BIDDLE SHIPMAN

JUDITH B. TANKARD

A History of Women in
Landscape Architecture
by Leslie Rose Close

SAGAPRESS, INC.

In Association With
THE LIBRARY OF
AMERICAN LANDSCAPE HISTORY, INC.

Distributed By
HARRY N. ABRAMS, INC.

The Library of American Landscape History, a not-for-profit corporation, was founded in the belief that clear, informative books about American landscape design will broaden support for enlightened preservation. Library publications are intended for landscape historians, members of the profession, and the interested public. *The Gardens of Ellen Biddle Shipman* is the second volume in the Designers and Places series.

The board of directors thanks the LALH editorial advisers: Keith N. Morgan, Boston University; Catha Grace Rambusch, Wave Hill; David C. Streatfield, University of Washington; William H. Tishler, University of Wisconsin—Madison; and Suzanne L. Turner, Louisiana State University. We are particularly grateful for the generous research and production subsidies that have helped bring this book to print.

Nancy R. Turner, President; John Franklin Miller, Clerk; Eleanor G. Ames, Treasurer; and Nesta Spink.

The Gardens of Ellen Biddle Shipman
Copyright © 1996 by Sagapress, Inc., Sagaponack, New York
All rights reserved.
Distributed by Harry N. Abrams, Inc., New York
A Times Mirror Company

Photographs of the gardens of Ellen Biddle Shipman on pages ii, vi, viii, xi, xii, xx, 182, and jacket front copyright © 1996 by Carol Betsch
Edited by Carol Betsch
Design and Composition by Greg Endries
Production coordinated by Carol Lewis
Printed in Hong Kong

Library of Congress Cataloging-in-Publication Data

Tankard, Judith B.
    The Gardens of Ellen Biddle Shipman / Judith B. Tankard.
        p.   cm.
    "A history of women in landscape architecture by Leslie Rose Close."
    Includes bibliographical references (p. 213) and index.
    ISBN 0-89831-033-4 (Sagapress). — ISBN 0-8109-4466-9 (Abrams)
    1. Shipman, Ellen. 2. Women landscape architects—United States—-Biography. 3. Landscape architects—United States—Biography. 4. Landscape architecture—United States. 5. Gardens—United States—Design.   I. Library of American Landscape History. II. Title.
SB470. S48T36   1996
712' .092—dc20
[B]   96-1667
                                                                          CIP

Your [garden] plan is the key that will open the door into a new world—
a world where many of the great people of the earth, rich and poor,
high and low, have worked and slaved to recreate the beauty that
man has so often destroyed, into the paradise it was meant to be.

—ELLEN BIDDLE SHIPMAN,
Garden Note Book

Garden Door

An exhibition titled
The Gardens of Ellen Biddle Shipman,
which includes photographs from this book,
has been made possible by
PaineWebber Group, Inc., and the Parrish Art Museum.
A grant from the National Endowment for the Arts
will enable it to travel.

CONTENTS

FOREWORD

THIS PROJECT was initiated many years ago by Daniel Krall, associate professor of landscape architecture at Cornell University, where the majority of Ellen Biddle Shipman's archives are housed. Krall had researched Shipman and her gardens for almost a decade before illness forced him to put aside his work. He then contacted the Library of American Landscape History with an invitation to assume development of his monograph. We, in turn, approached Judith B. Tankard, landscape historian and founding editor of the *Journal of the New England Garden History Society*, who had written extensively about the gardens of the British designer Gertrude Jekyll.

It soon became apparent that the near-complete lack of Shipman's personal and professional correspondence would preclude writing the full-scale biography Krall had once envisioned. We opted instead for an interpretive essay on Shipman's major garden work, presented in the context of her life and times. Tankard was inspired by the quality of Shipman's design projects recorded in hundreds of plans, photographs, and drawings in the collection of Cornell University Libraries and intrigued by the details of her life. Additionally, Shipman's success in the male-dominated profession despite her status as a divorced, working mother offered an opportunity to reflect on issues beyond those of aesthetics and style.

Because of the large scope of Shipman's oeuvre, a representative selection of her gardens is presented. And, in the interest of readability, the text offers a distillation of Shipman's ideas rather than a comprehensive view of each design. Some gardens are presented in horticultural detail; some are explored from architectural or spatial perspectives; others provide a window onto interesting relationships with clients. Most of Shipman's gardens have changed dramatically since they were constructed and planted, and few opportunities exist to experience her art firsthand. We are especially pleased to be able to feature one fine exception—the English Garden at Stan Hywet Hall, which has recently been restored to Shipman's original planting plans. John Franklin Miller, former executive director of the site, has described the drama of this restoration in an Afterword.

The editors and board of the Library of American Landscape History believe that thorough yet lively books about landscape history have the potential to encourage increasingly thoughtful stewardship of gardens such as those Ellen Shipman designed. We are also hopeful that this book may contribute to a richer understanding of women of the early twentieth century and their relationship to work. Many readers will undoubtedly be struck by the discrepancy between Shipman's formidable accomplishments and her decision to obliterate the records that would have protected her work from the near oblivion into which it fell. It has been extremely satisfying to rediscover Ellen Shipman's garden designs and bear witness to a remarkable achievement.

The Library of American Landscape History, Inc., is indebted to the Akron Garden Club for their generous support of this project and to the Graham Foundation for Advanced Studies in the Visual Arts, the Helen S. Wolle Foundation, the Hubbard Educational Trust, and Nancy Angell Streeter for their financial assistance in realizing this book. We are also grateful to individuals who have read and made helpful comments on the manuscript: Leslie Rose Close, Valencia Libby, Diane Kostial McGuire, John Franklin Miller, Ngaere Macray, Keith N. Morgan, and Suzanne L. Turner. A special note of thanks to our editor, Carol Betsch.

Robin Karson, Executive Director
Library of American Landscape History

The Gardens of Ellen Biddle Shipman

INTRODUCTION

A History of Women in Landscape Architecture
Leslie Rose Close

ON THE TRAGIC march of the Trail of Tears, Navaho women "clung to the seeds and roots they had dug from their gardens before being driven from their homes." And for pioneer women moving West, the scorched tracts of arid land awaiting them did not "blossom like the rose," but, carefully tended, they could offer limited beauty—and memories of what had been left behind.[1] Women have had a long association with agriculture and horticulture in America. Native American women were the trustees of the seeds, cuttings, and rootstocks through many difficult migrations. Colonists venturing into the New World also brought the vines and seeds that would remind them of home: "What must that sweet air from the land have been to the sea-weary Puritan women on shipboard, laden to them with its promise of a garden! For I doubt not every woman bore with her across seas some little package of seeds and bulbs from her English home garden, and perhaps a tiny slip of plant of some endeared flower, watered each day, I fear, with many tears."[2]

The identification of women with gardens reflects a larger, gendered split in domestic territory. The house, its structure, placement, and maintenance have traditionally been the male domain, while the household interior and the surrounding grounds have been women's.[3] Originating in the notion of woman as nurturer, provider of beauty, and nest-builder, these associations often have been extended to the belief that women are temperamentally suited to horticultural pursuits, that they are in fact endowed with "natural" talents in this area. By the nineteenth century, the upper classes in the United States came to see an artistic devotion to "domestic beautification" as a sign of breeding and good taste, a patrician aspect of garden design that endures to the present. In the early decades of the twentieth century, articles on garden design most often appeared on the society pages of the newspaper; today one is likely to find society news within articles on gardens.

During the last half of the nineteenth century, an influential "how-to" literature written and consumed by women helped foster the idealization of women's roles. Jane Loudon's *Gardening for Ladies* (1840), Ella Rodman Church's *The Home Gardener* (1881), and Celia Thaxter's *An Island Garden* (1894) were among many books available and avidly read. Mariana van Rensselaer's *Art Out-of-Doors, Hints on Good Taste in Gardening,* published in 1893, brought the imprimatur of aristocratic authority to horticultural pursuits and fostered the notion of American landscape design as an art form.[4] Gardening was also defined as a source of solace for women, a "distraction from the unavoidable disappointments and trials of life."[5]

Although stereotyped and, by today's standards, retrograde, these "ladies' books" did help promote a professional role for women in architecture and landscape architecture. Harriet Beecher Stowe, who designed her own Connecticut house in 1863, may have been one of the first to voice the opinion that "architecture and landscape gardening are arts in every way suited to the genius of woman," adding that "there are enough that have the requisite mechanical skill and mathematical education" to elevate these domestic pursuits to a profession.[6]

The education of women in landscape architecture closely followed the establishment of the field's first professional organization, the American Society of Landscape Architects, in 1899. (Among its eleven founding members was one woman, Beatrix Jones—later Farrand—niece of the novelist Edith Wharton.) In 1901, the Lowthorpe School of Landscape Architecture for Women was founded by Judith Motley Low, who echoed the widespread belief that "women were naturally adapted to this profession."[7] Nine years later, the Pennsylvania School of Horticulture for Women at Ambler opened its doors; its first co-director was a woman, Louise Bush-Brown. One of the most influential and highly regarded new programs, the Cambridge School of Architecture and Landscape Architecture for Women, was founded in 1916. It had begun a year earlier as a tutorial program operated from the office of landscape architect Bremer Pond and architect Henry Atherton Frost, two young Harvard instructors who believed that "women turn more naturally [than men] to landscape work."[8] The flexible and somewhat unconventional approach applied at the Cambridge School reflected the notion that architecture and landscape architecture should be collaborative rather than competitive disciplines. Frost and Pond created a course of study in which students in both tracks followed almost identical programs. Ellen Biddle Shipman's early training in the office of architect Charles Platt was similarly oriented.

The Gardens of Ellen Biddle Shipman

By the early 1920s (the time when Ellen Shipman moved her practice to New York), landscape design was widely considered a viable career for women. Ironically, overdrawn female stereotypes and rigidly proscribed gender roles may actually have facilitated the professionalization of women in the field. Like nursing, the education of children, and social work—the few occupations historically open to women—a career in gardening and landscape design could be accepted as a logical extension of women's traditional domestic roles. *What Girls Can Do* (1926) was one of several publications to suggest that a young woman with "an artistic sensibility and a love of things that will grow" could become a landscape gardener. To this end, she was advised to attend a good school of horticulture and train for the "delightful work ... [of] creating a beautiful garden around a beautiful house."[9] Residential landscape design was not the only specialization envisioned for women. The author of the 1924 *Profitable Vocations for Girls* suggested that landscape gardening and interior decoration could be extended to the laying out of parks, grading and terracing, and the supervision of gardening staff.[10] In reality, however, Shipman and many of her colleagues found entry into public work exceedingly difficult.

Despite increasing opportunities for education and, to some degree, employment, considerable obstacles to success remained for women in landscape architecture, as in all professions. When Frederick Law Olmsted Sr. described Beatrix Farrand as one who was "supposed to be in some way inclined to dabble in landscape architecture," he was echoing pervasive sentiments.[11] And it is instructive to remember that Olmsted was a progressive humanist, one of the most forward-thinking men of his day. It is also instructive to realize that twenty years later, when women had firmly established their presence and potential in the profession, the Third National Conference on Instruction in Landscape Architecture held at Cornell University resolved that women students in landscape architecture be required to take a stenography course, as the skill would be most useful in helping them to secure work in professional offices.

Many young women continued to find their career progress impeded in fundamental ways. The traditional path for male landscape architects was a postgraduate apprenticeship for several years in an established office, during which time new skills were mastered and contacts made for future work. After learning the business of running a firm, the young practitioner would then venture out into solo or joint practice or go into one of the large national firms, such as Olmsted Brothers Associates. This route was closed to women graduates, who found themselves barred from apprenticeship positions. The prevailing prejudices that excluded women from male-owned offices were twofold. First, it was widely believed that the mere presence of women "disrupted the morale" in an all-male office. Additionally, women were viewed as not having the personal authority or the managerial skills to supervise construction, and it was felt that men, especially in construction crews, would balk at direction from a woman.[12]

For many of the women who pioneered the field, one answer was to create paths of their own and, for some, to provide a route for other women. Marian Coffin, who became one of the most accomplished designers of her generation, was unable—even after completing studies at MIT—to find a position in a firm; she had to open her own office. Ellen Shipman trained with Charles Platt but opened her own office early in her career without ever having worked for a landscape architecture firm. Beatrix Farrand, encouraged by her mentor Charles Sargent of the Arnold Arboretum, also entered the field early and ran her own office. As did Shipman, Farrand hired women exclusively. Their commitment to giving women an entry into the profession had a far-reaching effect on women's presence in the field. Several Shipman and Farrand employees went on to develop their own practices and partnerships; several carried on the tradition of hiring only women.

Within the profession, there was a tacit, and limiting, gender-defined division of labor. Even when working with established firms, women often found themselves relegated to designing planting plans. Shipman's first collaborations with Charles Platt followed this pattern. Perhaps its ultimate expression was the "married partnership" of a female landscape architect and a male architect, which emerged during this period. Among these husband-and-wife "teams" were Ruth Dean and Aymar Embury, Janet Darling and Richard Webel, Agnes Selkirk Clark and Cameron Clark, and Helen Morgenthau Fox and Mortimer Fox. Business considerations no doubt played an important role in the arrangement, in which the husband was naturally viewed as the head of the company—a perception that sidestepped widespread biases against women in business and against doing business with women. Additionally, the resistance often encountered by women supervising construction crews could be circumvented by having husband-partners assume this role.

Women's eventual success in landscape architecture was fostered, certainly, by the tremendous growth in opportunities for the entire profession, especially in domestic design. In 1915, the American Academy in Rome established the first three-year fellowship in landscape architecture, elevating it to an equal status with painting and architecture. The National Park Service was established in 1916. City and community planning soon became the active concern of landscape architects. The vast fortunes of America's new capitalists were financing legions of elaborate estates. From the 1880s until World War II, a period identified as the Country Place Era, lavish grounds and formal gardens became their celebrated features. The Beaux Arts approach taken by the architects of the mansions suggested European models for the design of the gardens. Spatial layouts in

The Gardens of Ellen Biddle Shipman

the French, Italian, and Spanish styles, with stonework, topiary, parterres, iron-work, statuary, fountains, and pools, were the rage. An English style, with attendant romantic rose and perennial gardens, was favored for so-called summer cottages in areas such as Southampton, Long Island.

The new estates and their gardens were published in scores of magazines, books, and journals. Photography, a relatively new feature of these publications, did much to fuel the garden mania of the 1910s and 1920s. Many of the period's best photographers were women. Mattie Edwards Hewitt, Frances Benjamin Johnston, Jessie Tarbox Beals, Antoinette Perrett, and others made their careers by photographing new work of a rising generation of landscape architects. Their photographs illustrated the garden and architectural periodicals, professional journals, and books that both drove and documented this period of extravagant residential design.[13]

By the 1920s, an intricate network had developed of professional women authors, landscape architects, and photographers who did much to champion women in the field of residential design. One of the most prominent was Louisa Yeomans King, writing under the name Mrs. Francis King, who helped found both the Women's National Farm and Garden Association and the Garden Club of America. King's articles—many of which praised the work of Ellen Ship-man—appeared in newspapers as well as in periodicals. Her popular books were aimed specifically at upper-middle-class readers, although her *Pages from a Garden Notebook*, published in 1921, was introduced at a dormitory opening for women students at Massachusetts Agricultural College (now the University of Massachusetts), in Amherst. King's advocacy of women's participation in farm- and garden work helped promote a new definition of their capacity for physical work outside the home.

The profession, however, still struggled for an identity. In Louise Shelton's *Beautiful Gardens in America* (1915), many of the grandest estate gardens of the period are described in elaborate detail, but not a single landscape architect is mentioned by name. In an increasingly common manifestation of client vanity, the owners of the estates are credited with the "good taste" to have created such extraordinary settings. That many of the uncredited landscape architects were women suggests a gender bias underlying this much-repeated oversight.

The stock market crash in 1929 slowed building considerably; increasingly fewer and smaller estates were built during the Depression. These more modest homes and developments did not demand elaborate landscapes, and often the services of landscape architects were not required. With project loads reduced, many offices closed and others drastically cut their staffs. The larger landscape architecture firms that remained intact moved toward public work as the profession began a dramatic reorganization in response to the government's new role as its major employer. Some women found work in programs such as the Civilian Conservation Corps, but competition for government agency jobs was intense and the discrimination formidable. Women were at a distinct disadvantage when competing with men for public projects.

During the Great Depression, disapproval of working women increased as they were perceived as robbing men of the few available jobs. A Gallup poll conducted in 1936 reported that 82 percent of all Americans felt that wives should not work if husbands were able. When Henry Frost approached the editor of *American Architect* with an article he had written promoting the hiring of women landscape architects, "the explosion was immediate." As he related, "My editor friend told me forcefully that he would not be guilty of lifting his hand to help the cause of women in any fields that belonged by rights to men. He harangued on the way women were forcing themselves into business and professional circles everywhere. One statement I have never forgotten. 'The subways of New York are filled with ticket-takers and track walkers who hold degrees from our leading law schools, and are forced to do such menial labor by the influx of women into their profession.' I was ushered out, or should I say driven from his office with hardly an opportunity to pick up my hat."[14]

After the Depression, landscape architecture, despite its elite foundations, was redefined as embracing a more public mission. The Garden Club of America reflected the shifting emphasis. Its first annual competition in 1917 had been for the design of a flower garden; by 1933, the competition had been refocused on the design of a small suburban development. Park design, conservation, and planning became major sources of work for landscape architects under the auspices of the Tennessee Valley Authority, the National Capital Parks and Planning Commission, and the National Park Service (which employed the greatest number of landscape architects during the 1930s but was not known for hiring women). The New York City Parks Department under Robert Moses, however, hired forty landscape architects, including many women—Helen Bullard, Maud Sargent, and Helen Swift Jones among them—to develop a rehabilitation program for city parks.

Within a short time, parks, campus planning, parkway design, community planning projects, and conservation programs had almost completely replaced estate design as the primary sources of work for landscape architects. Sadly, few women made a successful transition from estate design to public work.[15] Ellen Shipman's efforts to bridge the gap between private and public work during the lean years of the late 1930s met with some success, but her lack of training in site planning precluded her involvement in the sorts of projects where Marjorie Sewell Cautley, Helen Bullard, and a small number of other women found jobs.

The Gardens of Ellen Biddle Shipman

Nevertheless, by the 1930s, women had achieved a highly visible success in the profession and their work appeared regularly in popular and professional periodicals. By 1935, it was even possible for some critics to suggest that women landscape practitioners may have met with more success than men. "Women Take Lead in Landscape Art; Field Is Dominated by a Group of Brilliant Designers of Horticultural Vistas" was the title of a *New York Times* article on 13 March that year. Between 1929 and 1936, three women won the Architectural League of New York's highest awards for landscape architecture: Ruth Bramley Dean was awarded the Medal of Honor for gardens in Grosse Pointe, Michigan, in 1929; Marian Coffin's designs for Mrs. T. Morgan Wing and Mr. and Mrs. Edgar Bassick brought her the Medal of Honor in 1930; and in 1932, Annette Hoyt Flanders won for the "French Gardens" on the McCann estate in Oyster Bay, Long Island. In 1938, *House and Garden* pronounced Shipman "Dean of American Women Landscape Architects," despite her having never received a formal award.

Although there was not much landscape work undertaken during World War II, the war had a positive effect on the perception of women in the work place. As wartime labor shortages demanded that manual labor for women be viewed positively, Rosie the Riveter was offered to the American public in counterpoint to previous stereotypes. College admissions were also increasingly open to women, many of whom experienced a new freedom in occupational mobility. The end of the war, however, brought the return of the troops and a return to old standards. A tremendous backlash drove many of women out of the work force and back into the home. The GI Bill also had the effect of discouraging women in university programs and fueling the general bias against women in the work place.

Ellen Shipman and other women landscape architects achieved remarkable success given the obstacles they faced. They established themselves in a highly competitive male profession that was particularly unwelcoming in a time of social, political, and economic upheaval in the United States. We have only just begun to document women's specific design contributions and to analyze their profound influence on the profession—and, conversely, the degree to which their involvement was shaped by contemporary attitudes. It is not surprising that Ellen Shipman's professional story begins with her own redefinition of the roles of wife and mother as they were traditionally experienced.

THE GARDENS OF
ELLEN BIDDLE SHIPMAN

Ellen Shipman in Poins House garden. Nancy Angell Streeter Collection

CHAPTER ONE

EARLY YEARS

WARREN MANNING considered her "one of the best, if not the very best, Flower Garden Maker in America." In 1933, *House and Garden* hailed her as the "dean of American women landscape architects." *House Beautiful* regularly featured her projects in their column "Gardens in Good Taste." A 1950 obituary in the *New York Times* identified her as "one of the leading landscape architects of the United States."[1] At the peak of her career, Ellen Biddle Shipman worked on projects as far-flung as Long Island's Gold Coast and Seattle; York Harbor, Maine, and New Orleans. Her clients included Fords, Astors, du Ponts, and Seiberlings, captains of industry, financial leaders, and patrons of the arts. At her death, she had completed over six hundred projects.[2]

After a period of informal apprenticeship with the architect Charles A. Platt, Ellen Shipman established her own practice. Throughout her career, she continued to work both independently and in collaboration with Platt and other prominent architects and landscape architects. Today's view of Shipman focuses almost exclusively on her ability to design plantings that "softened" the architectural "bones" laid out by her partners, but her artistic achievements were considerably more extensive. In the hundreds of gardens for which she designed both plantings and architectural elements, Shipman arrived at her own distinctive style. In her solo work her imagination found freer, arguably more vital expression.

Domesticity, intimacy, and romantic, sensual seclusion characterized the best of Ellen Shipman's landscape designs, distinguishing them from the grander, self-consciously European schemes that were commonplace during the period. Shipman's own experiments with large-scale European-influenced estate design generally do not figure among her most memorable work. Her more original aesthetic derived from the quiet simplicity of traditional Colonial-revival spatial layout, the convention of the outdoor room, an artist's approach to planting, and a sense of the garden as a lush, green, and—above all—private world. Her debt to the British designer Gertrude Jekyll is unmistakable, but Shipman's gardens were American in spirit and impact.

Shipman's career depended on the same booming economy that kept her colleagues busy with prominent, large-scale jobs. And like her colleagues, she was well aware of the fundamental task at hand: to create evocative backdrops for her wealthy clients' social lives. But Shipman was first and foremost a gardener, and it was from personal experience that she approached landscape design. "The renaissance of the art," Shipman wrote, "was due largely to the fact that women, instead of working over their boards, used plants as if they were painting pictures and as an artist would."[3]

Shipman wanted all homeowners to experience the excitement of gardening firsthand and lectured widely on topics ranging from color, layout, and maintenance to planting design. She wrote a gardening book that was intended for a middle-class audience, but postwar shifts in taste and homeowners' attitudes precluded its publication. Shipman's view of gardening was emphatically democratic, as one passage in her preface eloquently expresses: "Gardening opens a wider door than any other of the arts—all mankind can walk through, rich or poor, high or low, talented and untalented. It has no distinctions, all are welcome."[4]

Shipman was also an active advocate for women in the profession. For over thirty-five years she ran an all-women office where she trained many successful designers. She also served as an adviser to the Lowthorpe School of Landscape Architecture and Horticulture for Women in Groton, Massachusetts, and frequently in her lectures and in interviews emphasized the importance of women. She believed that women were crucial to the gardening revival that enlivened the century's early years. "Before women took hold of the profession," she wrote, "landscape architects were doing what I call cemetery work.... Until women took up landscaping, gardening in this country was at its lowest ebb."[5]

Shipman viewed home and garden as an almost hallowed sanctuary, perhaps as a result of her own geographically dislocated childhood. Vivid recollections reveal an image of the garden as the very essence of domesticity. "Our memory of our childhood home is not the architecture of the house, but the fragrance of the lilac, lily of the valley, jasmine, or the blooming of the rose," she later noted. About one such early moment at her grandparents' house, she reminisced: "Looking through a high white washed paling fence, I saw a white lilac in bloom with rose, tulips and forget-me-nots at its feet. The picture remains with me still and I only have to call it to mind to feel again the thrill of that May morning."[6] The lasting impression left by the image would inspire her to create a lifetime of such garden pictures.

The apparent contradiction inherent in this formative garden scene—at once unassuming and "thrilling"—was echoed by paradoxes in Shipman herself. She was, on the one hand, a down-to-earth, at times even deferent, designer, eager to satisfy her clients' most specific horticultural requests and to create gardens that blended seamlessly with the landscape beyond. She accepted tightly constrained commissions that many other designers would have refused, jobs that were limited to planting only or to borders within larger landscapes by other landscape architects. But Shipman's bearing was commanding, her presence determined, charismatic, even regal. Handsome, tall, articulate, and utterly sure of her own tastes, she exerted authority among her wealthy clients and ran one of the most successful practices in New York. Despite Shipman's reknown and the exactitude of her garden schemes, however, most of them proved ephemeral. That their character derived so specifically from horticultural rather than architectural determinants made them especially vulnerable to the ravages of time, disease, and changing tastes. Shipman watched most of her designs disappear within years of their implementation.

As a divorced, working mother at a time in history when societal support for neither circumstance existed, Ellen Shipman faced a set of extraordinarily difficult challenges. And as her career gained momentum, professional aspirations forced a series of decisions that jeopardized the very domestic pleasures her gardens so idyllically expressed. Ellen Shipman triumphed against great odds to make beautiful gardens, but that success did not come without its personal price.

Ellen McGowan Biddle was born on 5 November 1869 in Philadelphia, the daughter of Ellen Fish McGowan Biddle from Elizabeth, New Jersey, and Colonel James Biddle, a career soldier from the Philadelphia branch of the family, a large and powerful clan who counted among their houseguests the Prince of Wales.[7] Ellen's parents and two brothers were living at a military outpost in Brenham, Texas, when Mrs. Biddle returned east to give birth to her daughter. Despite an early bout of enteric fever, the baby thrived, and mother and daughter soon rejoined the rest of the family.

Ellen's adventurous childhood was spent at frontier outposts in Nevada, Colorado, and the Arizona Territory, where she rode horses and played with children in the local tribes. Mrs. Biddle remembered her daughter during these years as "happy as a bird."[8] On family expeditions through canyons and valleys, the family camped out in the desert, where Ellen saw mesquite and acacia trees of commanding size and cactus of every description. Buffalo and antelope grazed

Ellen McGowan Biddle and Colonel James Biddle. From *Reminiscences of a Soldier's Wife* (Philadelphia, 1907)

western plains flooded by crimson sunsets, while sudden storms and plagues of grasshoppers offered reminders of nature's capriciousness. Vegetation on the desert edge was especially precious. Ellen remembered "the excitement of seeing water that my father had ordered brought for miles to a Nevada post...to feed the trees he had planted along the driveways—the only trees in our vicinity."[9]

Not all Shipman's early memories were of wilderness, however. She also reveled in the glitter of military balls and festive dinners during the Colonel's leaves in San Francisco and, when an uprising of the local tribe threatened the family's safety, she came east with her mother and brothers for an extended visit with her grandparents. As the train approached the McGowans' New Jersey farm, four-year-old Nelly pointed out the window to the "beautiful stones growing out there." She had never seen grave markers before and assumed they had sprouted in the grass.[10] Her children's excitement at seeing cultivated fruit and real gardens for the first time delighted Mrs. Biddle.

The family was reunited on the frontier once tensions were quelled. At the age of six, when her older brothers were sent to school in Connecticut, Ellen was left to amuse herself in Fort Whipple, Arizona Territory. Ellen's mother noted that her daughter "was quite tall for her age, rode well, and was perfectly fearless, also hearty and strong, owing to the outdoor life in that wonderful climate."[11] Four

The Gardens of Ellen Biddle Shipman

years later, she too was dispatched east for school, as her parents felt she should find companionship of girls her own age. She went reluctantly.

Life in New Jersey offered lasting though comparatively tame pleasures and a more traditional social environment. Ellen's grandmother was "a lover of flowers, plants and shrubs, and of working among them." Shipman later recalled the joy of "finding a real garden" at her grandparents, where "it was impossible not to pick flowers and to break fast rules—a rose to hold all the way to school seemed well worth the punishment." She credited both her father and her grandparents for instilling in her "a great love of growing things."[12] The contrast between the starkness of the West and the green fertility of New Jersey made a strong impression on the young girl. While her earliest memories were set against the backdrop of mountains and desert, her first sense of "garden" came from trips east, where cultivated flowers and white picket fences must have seemed almost toylike in comparison to the grandeur, and danger, of the West. Throughout her career, Shipman retained a notion of the garden as artifice and haven, an embellishment, rather than an abstraction of nature.

During her teenage years, Ellen was sent to finishing school at Miss Sarah Randolph's in Baltimore, where her strong artistic gifts emerged and were celebrated. After finding the margins of Ellen's school notebooks "full of house plans and garden plans of all descriptions," Miss Randolph gave her an architectural dictionary as a history prize. Shipman later remembered the importance of the gesture. Miss Randolph had seen her talent years before she recognized it herself.[13]

In 1887, when Ellen was eighteen, her parents moved to Washington, D.C., where Colonel Biddle was reassigned to the War Department. Mrs. Biddle's reminiscences offer little information about this period, other than noting that her daughter had "tasted to the full during the two years in Washington all that a society life could give her."[14] How she spent the intervening years is unknown, but by the early 1890s Ellen was living in Cambridge, Massachusetts, in a rented house with a group of women friends, an unconventional arrangement that would have been discouraged in more conservative Baltimore. Among these friends were Mary Lucy Wilkins Rogers, Louise Emory, and Marian Nichols, who later provided important connections for Shipman's subsequent career as a landscape architect. (Marian's younger sister, Rose Standish Nichols, was to become a well-known landscape architect and writer; Margaret Nichols, Marian's other sister, would marry the landscape architect Arthur Shurcliff—then Shurtleff—whose professional path would intersect with Shipman's.)[15]

Only one record of Ellen's 1892–93 enrollment at Radcliffe, then known as Harvard Annex, survives to document a rather undistinguished and shortlived academic career.[16] Family lore suggests that she may have been involved in suffrage

Ellen Biddle in Boston, c. 1890. Photo Marshall. Nancy Angell Streeter Collection

activities during this time.[17] Perhaps she was distracted from her studies by her housemate Mary Rogers's cousin, Louis Evan Shipman.[18] Louis was charming and lively with literary aspirations, the son of a New York City contractor, descended from a well-established upstate New York family.[19] He had attended Brooklyn Polytechnic Institute before his only recorded term at Harvard. Like Ellen, he was twenty-three when he enrolled as a special student; also like Ellen, he withdrew after one year, in 1893.[20] The unlikely couple—photographs show her about half a head taller than he—were married that October at Ellen's parents' new home in Berkeley Springs, West Virginia. The Biddles, it seems, did not approve of the match.[21] The newlyweds soon moved to Connecticut, where Ellen gave birth the following August to a daughter, also named Ellen Biddle Shipman.

Ellen and Louis Shipman at Poins House, Plainfield, N.H. Nancy Angell Streeter Collection

CHAPTER TWO

LIFE IN THE CORNISH COLONY

IN THE SUMMER of 1894, Ellen and Louis visited Cornish, New Hampshire, a small village nestled in the mountains cradling the Connecticut River Valley.[1] Augustus Saint-Gaudens, uncle of Ellen's former housemate Marian Nichols, had discovered the village in 1885 and found its rural beauty irresistible. Imagining that it would be an ideal setting for his summer home and studio, he bought and "classicized" an old farmhouse there. Other artists soon followed, most of them fleeing the summer heat of New York City, where their artistic lives centered. Charles Platt came in 1889, and Thomas Dewing and his wife, the painter Maria Oakey Dewing, arrived in 1890; in 1893 Platt's friend Stephen Parrish, the Philadelphia painter and etcher, moved to the village community. The artists were followed by the literary glitterati and, over the years, by more ordinary folk.[2]

Ellen Shipman vividly remembered her first night in Cornish, during which she had attended a charade party at High Court, the home of the art patron Annie Lazarus. "The valley was still filled with rolling clouds... in the distance was Ascutney Mountain,... [and] just a few feet below, where we stood upon a terrace, was a Sunken Garden with rows bathed in moonlight of white lilies standing as an altar for Ascutney. As I look back I realize it was at that moment that a garden became for me the most essential part of a home. But," she added, "years of work had to intervene before I could put this belief, born that glorious night, into actual practice."[3]

For Ellen and Louis, then a promising playwright, life in an artists' colony offered freedom and opportunities for exchange with other creative souls. Their social life among the close-knit group of painters, sculptors, illustrators, writers, and musicians revolved around dinner parties and dramatic entertainments such as charades, there being little in the way of formal entertainment in the New Hampshire woods. They also liked masques, allegorical dramatic performances with costumed actors that provided opportunities for collaboration and high-spirited expression. The most famous of these was "A Masque of 'Ours,' The Gods and the Golden Bowl," given in 1905 in the pine grove below Saint-Gaudens's home, Aspet, during which Ellen Shipman assumed the role of Minerva, goddess of the arts and wisdom.[4]

But business took precedence over play in Cornish. Social calls were not encouraged before four o'clock, when the day's labors were complete. The only exceptions were "visits of state," when one artist invited another over for a critique or consultation. As one journalist observed in 1907, the atmosphere in Cornish was "one of culture and hard work."[5]

During their first two years there, the Shipmans shared a farmhouse with the writer and editor Herbert Croly and his wife, Louise. They then moved to nearby, less expensive Plainfield, where they rented an old brick tavern, which they named Poins House after a character in one of Louis's stories (whose revenue apparently paid the rent). Ellen made their attachment to the artists' colony obvious by playfully marking her calling cards "Geographically in Plainfield, Socially in Cornish."[6] "No one else thought of trying to live in [the house]," recalled one neighbor, "but the Shipmans, with their instinct for what could be made charming, saw its possibilities." Ellen had a knack for finding old furniture to outfit "rooms that seemed made for it."[7] She also created her first real garden there, a simple New England country garden with a dirt path lined with borders of traditional summer flowers, later lamenting that she never again had "such marvelous annuals." The ebullient borders set an informal, regional tone that was echoed in the low stone wall separating the garden from the road. The early, Colonial Revival design found a permanent place in Shipman's imagination and served as a prototype for many later projects.[8]

Much of the artistic energy in Cornish was devoted to horticulture, resulting in extraordinary gardens that affected not only Ellen Shipman but American garden design as a whole. She was well aware of the significance of what one critic identified as "the most beautifully gardened village in all America."[9] "Here," Shipman later wrote, "was the renaissance of gardening in America, the first effort in this country to return to early traditional gardening." She applauded the changes from a Victorian approach whose stiff artificiality clearly grated against her deepest aesthetic impulses: "The intricacy of the forms of beds, lying out in the lawn, was the predominant feature. These beds were filled with brilliantly colored small annuals—perennials and shrubs played no part. Frequently broken glass and colored pebbles were used to simulate flowers, as the flowers themselves could not be held permanently low enough to show the distorted designs. Privacy, imagination, and beauty had fled. This era of gardening almost, but not quite, killed the love of gardens."[10]

While many Cornish gardener-artists "hardly knew the commonest flowers by name," they were nevertheless thoroughly conversant with the principles of design—and their gardens showed it, attracting national attention as "livable, lovable spots, on very intimate terms with their owners."[11] The charm of these gardens lay in their unpretentious individuality, close visual and spatial ties to local vernacular architecture, and careful, sometimes passionate, maintenance: "One night when a number of us were dining with Maxfield Parrish," Shipman later remembered, "the talk had been so continually upon plants and diseases that he rose, put his hands on the table, and leaned over, said in a deep voice, 'Let us spray.' "[12]

Cornish artists had their transatlantic counterparts in Broadway, a picturesque village in the Cotswolds, made famous in the United States by Edwin Austin Abbey and other American illustrators for *Harper's Magazine*.[13] As in Cornish, many of the best Broadway gardens were designed by the artists who lived there, including several by Alfred Parsons, who portrayed them in paintings of winding walks, country cottages, and beds of old roses, hollyhocks, poppies, phlox, and other hardy plants growing in elegant, haphazard profusion.[14]

The rediscovery of hardy plants for American gardens was chronicled in many popular books at the turn of the century, including *A Woman's Hardy Garden* by Helena Rutherfurd Ely and Alice Morse Earle's *Old Time Gardens*.[15] Old-fashioned gardens flourished throughout the northeastern United States, from summer communities on Nantucket and in Easthampton, Long Island, to artists' colonies such as that at Old Lyme, Connecticut. Some were immortalized in paintings by resident artists, such as Maria Oakey Dewing, Stephen Parrish, and Edith Prellwitz in Cornish, and Childe Hassam, who painted gardens on Long Island and in Gloucester, Massachusetts. The quintessential old-fashioned flower garden was the tiny one created by the poet Celia Thaxter in Appledore, on the Isles of Shoals off the coast of Maine, made famous by Hassam's paintings and Thaxter's book, *An Island Garden*, published in 1894, just as Ellen Shipman arrived at Cornish.

The Cornish version of the "grandmother's garden" helped shape Ellen Shipman's aesthetic, while the highly sophisticated artists, architects, and critics she came to know there exposed her to the design techniques she needed to create it. Of these friends, the multi-talented Charles Platt exerted the most significant influence, but there were others, too, including Rose Standish Nichols, whose several books on travel and garden design remain classics; Herbert Croly, who became editor of the influential magazine *Architectural Record* and founder of *The New Republic;* the painter Stephen Parrish; and his son Maxfield Parrish, who illustrated Edith Wharton's book *Italian Villas and Their Gardens.*[16] Shipman also learned how to garden from her Cornish friends; Thomas Dewing's and other Cornishites' experiments with new varieties of hardy plants were avidly discussed by all.

Of the many gardens that were undoubtedly important in Shipman's development, two in particular stand out. Aspet, the summer home and studio of Augustus Saint-Gaudens, combined a classicizing renovation of a New England farm-

Edith Prellwitz, *Saint-Gaudens Garden* (Cornish, N.H.), oil on canvas, 1898. Saint-Gaudens National Historic Site

The Gardens of Ellen Biddle Shipman

Augusta Saint-Gaudens in garden at Aspet, Cornish, N.H., July 1906. Saint-Gaudens National Historic Site

house with several formal gardens. The gardens' strict axial geometry and lush plantings sounded two themes that later appeared in Shipman's own designs. Long after Saint-Gaudens's death, when Shipman had become a highly successful designer, she was commissioned to create a planting plan for the largest of these gardens.[17]

Shipman would also have known Northcote, Stephen Parrish's eighteen-acre estate sited on a steep Cornish hillside. Parrish had begun the garden in 1893 at the same time that he commissioned the residence from Wilson Eyre and just as the Shipmans were settling in the valley. "And such a garden!" one critic exclaimed. "Landscape painter for the fun of it, Stephen Parrish is a gardener for the love of it."[18] The horticultural elements of Parrish's rigorously studied "canvas" were subject to continual improvement and change, but the formal layout near the house, carefully framed views, and paths that meandered through the outlying shrubbery gave the garden its permanent structure. A garden enclosed on three sides by the vine-covered walls of the house was devoted to old-fashioned flowers, with raised beds featuring hardy roses, peonies, hollyhocks, and sweet william, interspersed

Stephen Parrish, *Northcote, Cornish, N.H.,* oil on canvas. Corporate Art Collection, The Reader's Digest Association, Inc.

with drifts of annuals. A blend of traditional and innovative elements made Parrish's garden one of the most memorable—amateur or professional—of the era.

The Shipmans were part of the small group of "chickadees" who lived year-round in Cornish. Henry and Lucia Fuller, Stephen Parrish, his niece Anne Parrish and son, Maxfield, and, later, the Saint-Gaudenses shared in the more intimate, more "truly Cornish" spirit that characterized the colony then. During long winter evenings, the release from gardening duties gave rise to active socializing. Frances Grimes, a sculptor who worked with Saint-Gaudens, remembered the Shipmans at one of many dinner parties they hosted: Louis, "the picture of hospitality ... rotund, beaming, with set phrases of greeting which could be anticipated. Ellen had a trace of southern manner; there was a sparkle in the gleam on her face which made her smile peculiarly hers. Nothing else was ever in their minds but your arrival." In October 1903 the couple celebrated their tenth anniversary at a surprise party planned by their friends, who came in costume with handmade gifts.[19]

The Gardens of Ellen Biddle Shipman

Louis's career took a promising turn when his play *D'Arcy of the Guards* opened to critical acclaim in San Francisco in 1901.[20] The saga of the dramatisation was the subject of one of his best books, *The Adventures of a Play*. Despite their richly creative life and the idyllic setting, however, problems began to surface in the Shipmans' household. The apparent root of these difficulties was financial—though he was enjoying critical success, Louis was not making much money as a writer. That Louis's life was increasingly centered in the literary world of New York while Ellen's interests were focused in the country may also have been a source of conflict. As Ellen grew closer to her Cornish neighbors, Louis alienated many, particularly those who did not know him well. Margaret Nichols Shurcliff's vivid memory of Louis during a tennis game captured the

Anne Parrish in garden at Northcote, Cornish, N.H., 1898. Saint-Gaudens National Historic Site

Life in the Cornish Colony   17

Louis Shipman near tennis court,
Brook Place, Plainfield, N.H.
Nancy Angell Streeter Collection

writer's intensity and self-absorption: a "fat roly-poly author and playwright ...
dripping with perspiration ... and pouring forth a continuous line of boasting
and teasing." His "absurdity is his safety," another friend recalled, adding,
somewhat ominously, "he is one that would bludgeon a lily before breakfast and
be proud of it all day." Yet another pegged Louis as "the warmest and most dele-
terious of friends, the bitterest and most innocuous of enemies."[21] Rumors of
Louis's wandering eye began to circulate. His absences from home became more
frequent. Within a few years, the marriage would deteriorate beyond repair.

While running the household increasingly on her own, Ellen continued to garden and dreamily to plan "innumerable houses for desirable and unprocurable
sites." She undoubtedly was encouraged by an event that had taken place in 1899,
when she and Louis were spending the winter in the home of Charles and Eleanor
Platt while awaiting the completion of renovation work at Poins House. On
returning from their yearly seasonal move to New York, Charles discovered some
house plans Ellen had inadvertently left behind on the drawing board in his studio. He penned her a note that said, "If you can do as well as I saw, you better keep
on," and made her a gift of a drawing board, T square, and drafting implements.[22]

However, none of Shipman's plans for "dream houses and dream gardens"
was realized until she and Louis purchased the John Gilkey farm in Plainfield,
around 1903. The late-eighteenth-century homestead on Meriden Stage Road

consisted of a cottage and a barn and was bordered by a mill brook that gave the property its name, Brook Place. The couple planned to remodel the farmhouse, located near the road, and live there until a new house was built farther back on the property to overlook Mt. Ascutney, but the Panic of 1907 killed the "grandiose idea," and instead, Ellen concentrated on a renovation that nearly doubled the modest size of the existing house.[23] (A small inheritence from her father, who died in June 1910, may have made the work possible.) Her plans were realized through Platt's office, but there is no evidence that Platt himself had any design involvement.[24]

Entrance hall, Brook Place, Plainfield, N.H. Photo Mattie Edwards Hewitt, 1923. Nancy Angell Streeter Collection

Garden, Brook Place. Photo Mattie Edwards Hewitt, 1923. Saint-Gaudens National Historic Site

The emotional significance of the project for Ellen was recorded in her unpublished Garden Note Book: "If you are planning to build a home, you are embarked on man's greatest achievement—it is for its protection that wars are fought; and for its beautification that other arts have been developed. It was the

The Gardens of Ellen Biddle Shipman

building of a home, one stone upon another, and the cultivation of the surrounding land that differentiated man from beast more than any other one thing.... Do not take this great experience casually—give it all the consideration such a momentous undertaking should receive."[25]

Shipman's orchestration of the architecture, interiors, and the layout of the grounds at Brook Place—which eventually comprised about two hundred acres—bore the mark of the refined, imaginative sensibility that friends and clients would soon seek out for their own properties. A large architectural addition transformed the modest farmhouse into a special dwelling with unusual charm. She added a large picture window with 120 curved panes of glass imported from England and paneling salvaged from a Vermont church. In the library a secret door led to Louis's private study overlooking the tiny brook, horse pastures, and hills beyond. In front of the house stretched a wide tree-lined lawn and, secluded from view, a tennis court. To the side of the house, beyond the pergola-shaded veranda, was Ellen's garden.

In her garden, Shipman refined and formalized the simple concepts she had explored at Poins House. It was the landscape's "charm, seclusion, and informality" that caught the eye of one writer, who observed that it harmonized "entirely with the dwelling."[26] Photographs by Mattie Edwards Hewitt taken in 1923 reveal the property at the peak of its development, but likely the plan began simply and evolved slowly in accordance with its maker's maturing tastes and her budget.[27] The garden functioned both as a setting for outdoor family life and as a learning laboratory for Ellen. "Working daily in my garden for fifteen years," she later wrote, "...taught me to know plants, their habits and their needs."[28]

Many Cornish gardens were featured in both the local and national press in those early years, but Shipman's was rarely among them. One mention in 1906 was confined to a notice of the "fragrant flowers of our grandmother's day" growing alongside the front path. The gardens most often singled out for praise were those more architecturally determined—the Dewings', Stephen Parrish's, Maxfield Parrish's, Saint-Gaudens's, and Annie Lazarus's High Court by Charles Platt.[29]

Platt was a landscape painter when he first arrived in Cornish as a summer resident in 1889, seeking solace after the tragic death of his young wife and their newborn twins. His first ideas about architecture were sparked by a trip to Italy in 1892 with his brother, William, a landscape architect and apprentice to Frederick Law Olmsted Sr., who warned William to ignore the "fine and costly gardens of Italy" in favor of the roadside scenery. Nonetheless, the brothers visited several villas and gardens, which Platt recorded in a brief text and haunting black-and-white photographs. These were first published as a series of articles,

Thomas W. Dewing, *Portrait of Charles A. Platt*, oil on canvas,
1893. Private Collection. Courtesy Saint-Gaudens National
Historic Site

then, in 1894, as a book, *Italian Gardens*. The strong resemblance of the Cornish Hills to the Tuscan landscape explains in part the colony's attraction for Platt.[30] But, from the beginning, Platt's intention was not to reproduce what he had seen in Italy but to adapt its spirit to an American context. As Royal Cortissoz noted in his introduction to his 1913 monograph on Platt: "A really typical Platt design has nothing alien about it. The old Italian idea is so tactfully and with such sincerity adjusted to local conditions that the completed work becomes part and parcel of a veritable characteristic American home."[31] Others were also convinced of the originality of Platt's designs and championed his work in contemporary journals. Among these influential writers was the Shipmans' neighbor Herbert Croly, for whom Platt would also design a home.

Platt's first professional Cornish commission was a house for Annie Lazarus, whose garden so inspired Shipman on her first visit.[32] No doubt Platt's training

The Gardens of Ellen Biddle Shipman

Flower garden at Villa Pamfili, 1894. From Charles A. Platt, *Italian Gardens* (New York, 1993). Courtesy Sagapress, Inc.

as a landscape painter helped him to visualize and control the all important views, especially the one to Mt. Ascutney, which he hid behind walls of hemlock until the visitor reached the rear courtyard. Terraces contained the sloping site and a modest flower garden was sited near the house. As at many Cornish houses, a grapevine-draped loggia was positioned for greatest enjoyment of the view to the mountains.

Over the years Platt also created houses for Herbert Adams, Winston Churchill (the novelist), Mary Banks Smoot, and other Cornishites. In 1890, he began his own simple clapboard house and studio, just below High Court, nestled in the Cornish Hills and overlooking the Connecticut River Valley. On his return from Italy in 1892, he added a loggia and gardens to enhance the visual connection with the landscape. Platt's integration of house and garden set the tone for a Cornish-based style that merged Italian concepts with vernacular form.

Charles A. Platt, *The Garden at High Court* (Cornish, N.H.), oil on canvas. Private Collection. Courtesy Saint-Gaudens National Historic Site

Platt's first design commission outside Cornish, landed in 1897, was in Brookline, Massachusetts, where he designed a large walled garden at Faulkner Farm for Charles and Mary Sprague. In addition to classical garden architecture—a pergola, a casino with flanking curved loggias, columns, and ornament—Platt introduced a flower garden, with overflowing beds of lilies, poppies, and phlox. An even grander commission for Platt followed in 1900 at The

The Gardens of Ellen Biddle Shipman

Weld, the home of Larz and Isabel Anderson. Though only one of several gardens on the large estate, the "Italian garden" was the most dramatic. A contemporary critic, Wilhelm Miller—the influential gardening editor of *Country Life in America*—quickly sensed the importance of Platt's achievement. To Miller's eye, Platt's garden was distinguished from other "Italianized" examples by the dominance, rather than the "merest incident," of flowers.[33]

The two-tiered arrangement of beds flanking the grassy central mall in the walled garden contained more than 17,000 square feet of bloom, providing continuous color from March to October. The combination of heavy architectural framework and massive floral display proved extremely photogenic and vaulted Platt to national prominence.[34] From then on, all his residential landscapes would feature lush, floriferous gardens. That his own talents did not include

Garden at The Weld, Larz Anderson estate, Brookline, Mass. Photo Thomas E. Marr, c. 1904.
Courtesy Society for the Preservation of New England Antiquities

Life in the Cornish Colony   25

Ellen Shipman with her son, Evan,
at Brook Place, c. 1906. Nancy
Angell Streeter Collection

planting design scarcely mattered; he would collaborate with specialists—such
as Ellen Shipman—to oversee this aspect of a project.

Like Platt, Shipman brought to her art a lively interest in gardening and architecture and a self-nurtured creative vision. And like Platt, her timing was fortu-
itous. Wealthy Americans throughout the country were seeking designers for
their new homes and gardens. But Shipman benefited from few of the advantages enjoyed by her female colleagues, including formal training and trips to
Europe. Limited financial resources prevented her from entering any of the several schools of landscape architecture in the New England area. In addition,
Shipman was a wife and mother, unlike most of the profession's women. Her
Cornish neighbor Rose Nichols was more typical of those who pursued careers
in landscape design in that she had the money and freedom to secure a formal
education and travel as she wished. After studying drawing with Platt and other
architects and visiting Europe, Nichols was admitted as a special student to the
Massachusetts Institute of Technology, where Marian Cruger Coffin, an even
more prominent woman in the field, was also trained.[35]

By 1908, Ellen and Louis had three children—young Ellen was followed by
Evan in 1904 and Mary four years later. Shipman tutored her children at home
because she did not find any of the eleven country schools in the Plainfield area
suitable for them. Her theories of education, recorded in a lone article on the
subject, reveal a firm sense of purpose and practicality: to inspire curiosity and to
direct a child's reasoning, rather than to supply the answers. She found the work
gratifying, and later recalled that for no other activity was she "so repaid as for

the few minutes each day that I have given to teaching my children."[36] During these years Shipman was also active in the Plainfield Mothers' and Daughters' Club, founded in 1897 to help needy families through the winter. The club also offered companionship to women and spearheaded a nationally recognized arts and crafts industry.[37]

In 1910 or thereabouts, Ellen Shipman decided to become a professional landscape architect. Her precise motivations are not recorded, but Louis's departure for London that year left the family without visible means of support. Other factors undoubtedly also played a role. Many of the women of Cornish worked in design- and art-related fields; additionally, landscape design was one of few professional options open to women at the time, and Shipman had friends and neighbors who were deeply involved in it. Rapid growth in the nation's economy was creating a large pool of potential clients clamoring for beautiful gardens. Charles Platt and other Cornish artists had ready access to this new world.

After Louis left, Ellen continued to maintain close friendships with many of her Cornish neighbors, particularly Charles Platt. It is likely that she also developed friendships with her clients, both men and women, but none are recorded

Ellen Shipman with Ellen, Evan, and Mary at Brook Place, c. 1910. Nancy Angell Streeter Collection

from these early years. She does not appear to have found another significant love relationship, at this point or any other in her lifetime, but the destruction of her personal papers has obscured many details of her emotional life. Shipman undoubtedly worked hard and spent considerable time alone as she was trying launch her business. Years later she wrote to a friend, "Each year—each day you spend alone only makes you see the future—I know—I have found work to be the only help—except my children and grandchildren."[38] As business consumed increasing amounts of Shipman's time, responsibility for running the household and caring for her two younger children, both still under ten years, fell to Ellen, her elder, adolescent daughter.[39] Had the Shipmans' daughter been unable to meet the emotional demands of the situation, her mother's professional life may well have taken an entirely different turn. Despite the cozy domesticity captured in the old photographs of Brook Place, Ellen Shipman had few opportunities for the more tranquil pleasures of motherhood.

CHAPTER THREE

COLLABORATION WITH CHARLES PLATT

SHIPMAN'S WORK with Platt began when he told her that "he liked the outcome of [her] efforts at Brook Place," and asked her "to do the planting for the places he was building." He well understood the importance of expert planting design to his own success, and Shipman had no doubts about the value of a Platt connection for her future career. But she was not quite prepared to take the leap: "I felt I could not [proceed] without further knowledge of expert drafting. He was good enough to permit one of his assistants to give me instruction." Shipman acknowledged that "it was working with Charles Platt and with his office that gave me the foundation for my future knowledge of design."[1]

The precise dates and details of Shipman's instruction are unknown, but correspondence indicates that she was actively working with Platt by 1913.[2] Given that the earliest surviving drawings from Shipman's own Cornish practice date from 1912, and that a letter from a friend that year referred to her happy engagement in the profession, it is likely that she began her apprenticeship about 1910, when she was forty-one.[3] Platt had achieved considerable national fame by that time; among his clients were wealthy industrialists from both coasts, including Harold F. McCormick, William G. Mather, and Russell Alger, and in 1913, the lavish monograph introduced by Royal Cortissoz was published, showing examples of Platt's architectural and landscape work.

Under the architect's tutelage, Shipman was exposed to a range of design experience and was soon preparing construction drawings for walls, pools, and

View from the terrace, Fynmere, James Fenimore Cooper estate, Cooperstown, N.Y., 1912. RMC-Cornell Univ. Library

small garden buildings. In a method similar to Shipman's own approach to teaching her children, Platt seems to have inspired his student's curiosity, directed her reasoning, and encouraged her to provide her own answers. He probably also gave her access to his professional library and encouraged her to build one of her own—by the 1920s, Shipman had assembled a fine collection of titles related to the profession. Like thousands of gardening enthusiasts across the country, she would have been eager for the information and images offered in well written and heavily illustrated new volumes. The combination of Platt's technical instruction and her exposure to a superb body of gardening literature accounts for Shipman's unusually strong start as a designer.

Among the British volumes that would have been available to her were *The Wild Garden* (1870) and *The English Flower Garden* (1883) by William Robinson, both of which emphasized the use of hardy plants. Gertrude Jekyll's *Color Schemes for the Flower Garden,* published in 1908 but not widely read in the United States until several years later, demonstrated an approach to planting design that stressed, for the first time, artistic arrangement—in Jekyll's words, "careful selection and definite intention." Inigo Triggs's books and Thomas Mawson's *Art and Craft of Garden Making* (1900) were also widely available.[4]

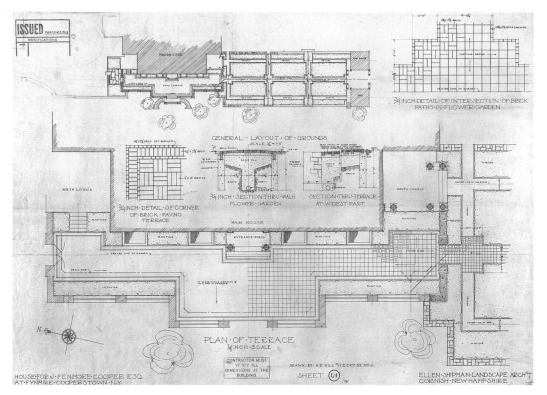

Plan of terrace drawn by Albert E. Hill, Cooper garden, ink on linen, 27 March 1913. RMC-Cornell Univ. Library

Accessible, too, were significant books on Italian design, more relevant to Shipman for their plans and architectural embellishments than for their plantings. Platt's own *Italian Gardens* appeared in 1894 and was followed ten years later by Edith Wharton's *Italian Villas and Their Gardens,* illustrated by Maxfield Parrish. Shipman could also have turned to many American publications for design and horticultural information. A tide of sophisticated gardening magazines bridged popular and professional concerns: *Garden and Forest, Country Life in America, House and Garden,* and *House Beautiful* had wide readerships. One of the most important American garden books of the day was Guy Lowell's *American Gardens* (1901), which featured work by Charles Platt.

The first documented collaboration between Platt and Shipman took place at Fynmere, the summer home of James Fenimore Cooper II in Cooperstown, New York. (Cooper was a lawyer who practiced in Albany and grandson of the famous author.) Platt was hired in 1913 to design an addition to the Frank P. Whiting house constructed three years previously and to enlarge the gardens. According to Platt's biographer, primary responsibility for the garden design was assigned to Shipman, who was supervised by her mentor.[5] By this stage of his career, Platt was interested in garden commissions only when he was also given jurisdiction over the design of the house.

Collaboration with Charles Platt   31

The Maiden of Fynmere by Herbert Adams, Cooper garden, 1912. Photo Slote Studio. RMC-Cornell Univ. Library

The small walled garden featured a broad terrace and a view of the Susquehanna River from an outlook embellished with patterned brickwork that recalled the terraces at Brook Place. Low stone walls allowed uninterrupted views to the distant hills and served to define the garden's edge. The garden's interior was filled with rectangular beds of flowers (specific varieties are not known) and a path system for circulation among them. A focal point was provided by fellow Cornishite Herbert Adams, who sculpted *The Maiden of Fynmere* for the garden. Shipman designed a toolshed-teahouse to echo the style of the residence and its material, local fieldstone. The sturdy, elegant building gave the gardener access to tools while the other side was left free for socializing. In subsequent projects, Shipman frequently used garden houses to define and focus space.

Apparently all did not go smoothly during the course of the commission. While the garden was under construction, Cooper declared that Shipman "had ruined" the place. "I had a feeling myself that I had," she confessed many years later. "There is an awful sinking feeling you can have...." Given her neophyte status, the substantial budget, and the fact that her mentor was looking over her shoulder, perhaps literally, Shipman must have been self-conscious, at the very least. Cooper demanded a driveway with room for a turnaround directly behind the house, but an existing road made the feature almost impossible. Even after she resolved the problem, Cooper would not acknowledge Shipman's input, claiming that he had "had all the ideas about doing it before [she] came."[6] The Coopers' son, however, expressed admiration for Shipman's work, remarking on the quality about it that would prove most enduring: "I think it was the most beautiful place I have ever seen—not grand but home-like and heart-warming."[7]

Still, the design was weak in comparison with Shipman's later work. She had not yet mastered the skills that would eventually enable her to create more authoritative three-dimensional spaces. The stone walls that defined the garden's edge were low in relation to the wide expanse of beds and walks and did not give

Garden houses under construction, Cooper garden, 1912. RMC-Cornell Univ. Library

Collaboration with Charles Platt   33

the garden the sculptural form necessary to achieve a distinct sense of place. The garden seemed almost a footnote to the big view beyond, its drafting-room genesis all too evident.

In 1914, Platt asked Shipman to design plantings for the James Parmelee estate near Washington Cathedral, in Washington, D.C., where two years earlier he had designed the house and adjacent walled garden.[8] Period illustrations reveal that Shipman's plantings—boxwood-edged beds filled with perennials, conical arborvitae, and roses on standards—did little to subdue Platt's rather relentless architectural framework. In fact, it seems that Shipman was following Platt's lead, emulating the formal rhythms of the architecture rather than counterbalancing it, as she soon would begin to do, with a richer, less orderly but more original planting style.[9]

Shipman faced other problems as a beginner. April 1914 found her in Ohio consulting with Platt's client William Gwinn Mather, who was displeased with the original plantings in the formal garden of his estate, Gwinn. Mather thought that the colors—determined by Paul Rubens Frost, Platt's young assistant—

Walled garden, The Causeway, James Parmelee estate, Washington, D.C., 1914. Photo Frances Benjamin Johnston, c. 1917. RMC-Cornell Univ. Library

The Gardens of Ellen Biddle Shipman

were too startling. Platt had recommended that Shipman visit Cleveland to rework the scheme. (Shipman was to receive several commissions to revise early planting designs.) Her suggestions for drift plantings in cool tones may have delighted Mather but they were disregarded by his gardener, as she discovered, to her exasperation, several weeks after her initial visit. "I regret extremely there should have been any misunderstanding as to what I am to do," she wrote Mather tersely, aware that she had not yet achieved unquestioned authority among clients and estate staff. By her next visit in June, Mather had managed to assuage Shipman's frustrations, but even so, nothing came of the scheme. It would be two decades before Shipman returned to Gwinn.[10]

One of the first artistically successful collaborations between Platt and Shipman was the Fahnestock garden in Katonah, New York, sometime after 1912. Olmsted Associates were originally hired to carry out planting plans in 1911 but were dismissed by the client in 1912. Platt, who was architect for the house, suggested Shipman as a replacement. Splendid photographs of the garden in maturity reveal that Shipman's planting composition was, this time, muscular enough to stand up to Platt's powerful architectural framework, dominated by an ornate, pedimented garden house.[11]

The interiors of the boxwood-bordered beds were filled with a rich mixture of perennials, flowering shrubs (including rhododendron), fruit trees, and conifers. Masses of individual plants and plant groups balanced the proportions of the broad walks, pool, and long vistas. One of the most evocative landscape passages on the property was an informal area developed behind the pavilion which resembled an Edwardian-era English kitchen garden. Rose trellises arched over a long path flanked by unruly borders of iris, poppy, lupine, and dianthus. By following this path, visitors could find the orchard and more naturalistic landscape beyond. Shipman and Platt were discovering a steady balance of purpose in their collaborations; their design skills were proving increasingly complementary.

When Platt was hired in 1915 to remodel the Georgian country home of Isaac T. Starr in the wealthy Chestnut Hill section of Philadephia, he again called on Shipman. Platt's symmetrical design used a loggia to link house and garden. Across a fifty-foot cruciform of two broad strips of turf stood a pergola of precisely the same dimensions as the loggia. It seems likely that Platt and Shipman decided together on the placement of architectural features and the overall planting scheme, for here dogwood, cedar, cherry trees, and shrubs were combined with groups of perennials to control views out of the garden and provide enclosure to a degree that Platt's independent designs did not. Again, Shipman's lush, loose plantings successfully evoked the spirit of Cornish gardens, even in this most formal of settings.

Collaboration with Charles Platt   35

Vista from pavilion, Girdle Ridge, William F. Fahnestock estate, Katonah, N.Y., c. 1912. Photo Jessie Tarbox Beals. RMC-Cornell Univ. Library

Pool and pavilion, Fahnestock garden, c. 1912. Photo Jessie Tarbox Beals. RMC-Cornell Univ. Library

The same year, 1915, found Shipman in Seattle, Washington, working on the Merrill garden Platt had designed six years before. The walled formal garden was a development of the style and layout Platt had introduced at The Weld and Faulkner Farm, but its general impression was less elaborate and less insistently architectural. Early photographs in the Platt monograph document the same rigorous drill plantings used at Gwinn. Shipman's charge, once again, was to enliven the geometric display. No photographs survive to record her work, but the Merrills retained Shipman's services over the next decade and a half.[12]

In the working methods they had forged, Platt and Shipman closely resembled their British contemporaries Edwin Lutyens and Gertrude Jekyll, whose partnership was well publicized and certainly known to Shipman. By 1912, Lutyens and Jekyll had completed many important projects that had been published in *Country Life* magazine, from which Shipman often clipped gardening articles. In 1913, the year the Platt monograph appeared, Country Life Library published a large folio on Lutyens's work, which elicited the comment from

Fahnestock garden, c. 1912. Photo Jessie Tarbox Beals. RMC-Cornell Univ. Library

Pool and loggia with *Pan*, Laverock Hill, Isaac T. Starr estate, Chestnut Hill, Pa. 1915. Photo Mattie Edwards Hewitt, c. 1924. RMC-Cornell Univ. Library

Shipman that the architect's "interesting and intricate patterns" for steps stressed the stonework more than plantings.[13] Lutyens and Jekyll's division of responsibilities varied from project to project, depending on the parameters of the job. Sometimes they worked together on design concept, frequently debating the placement of architectural features. At other times, they worked independently on separate tasks for the same project, but Jekyll always did the plantings. The Platt-Shipman partnership was likely not so collaborative but rather more reflective of the traditional, gendered division of labor by which men oversaw architectural tasks and women tended to planting design.

In 1919, a pivotal opportunity for Shipman to work on one of Platt's projects emerged in Grosse Pointe, Michigan. It was the first of forty-four design projects she would eventually do there. Her charge at the Russell A. Alger estate, The Moorings, was to revise Platt's planting scheme of about 1917 for the entrance court and a small pool garden. Photographs of the mature garden show mixed herbaceous and shrub plantings cradled in a dense evergreen backdrop and Platt's grapevine-covered pergola focusing a view to Lake St. Clair. They also

The Gardens of Ellen Biddle Shipman

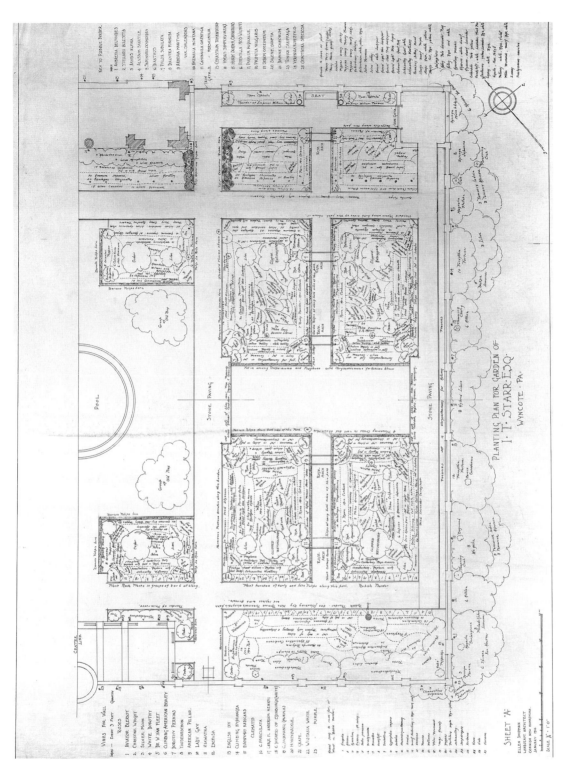

Planting plan, Starr garden, ink on linen, January 1916. RMC-Cornell Univ. Library

Path beside house, Starr garden, 1915. Photo Mattie Edwards Hewitt, c. 1924. RMC-Cornell Univ. Library

record Shipman's interest in linking the garden to the landscape beyond by merging the edge of the design with the surrounding landscape. Platt's recommendations for the Alger garden reveal his decidedly architectural orientation to plants. In specifying wild grape for the pergola, Platt noted that it had "a quality our domestic variety fails to possess; the leaves are very large, thin and translucent; they are lighter, brighter, more cheerful, and form ... a more graceful shelter."[14]

A fieldstone path alongside the Platt-designed residence was flanked by rich double herbaceous borders. Here the old-fashioned garden of Shipman's early years assumed greater sophistication. Standards of tea roses were backed by two varieties of lilies, white Japanese anemone, columbine, two varieties of monkshood, delphinium, and gas plant. By the late 1910s, Shipman routinely used the drift-style plantings promoted by Jekyll instead of the grid plantings she had specified in previous designs, such as those at Fynmere.

Around the rectangular pool, Shipman played groups of perennials against ascending layers of greenery to create a serene enclosure. The scale of plantings progressed from miniature to grand. At the pool's edge, tiny lustrous leaves of

The Gardens of Ellen Biddle Shipman

Garden wall, Starr garden, 1915. Photo Mattie Edwards Hewitt, c. 1924. RMC-Cornell Univ. Library

cotoneaster, then a recent import from China, provided a foreground for loose clumps of summer perennials and fruit tree standards. The setting deepened with small-scale ornamental shrubs and a backdrop of conifers.[15]

"Whatever type of garden," Shipman once observed, "in the background there should be a traditional copse or bosquet." Such a backdrop made the garden an intimate world-unto-itself. "This point cannot be too strongly stressed, and will be reiterated and reiterated," Shipman warned in her Garden Note Book, "…until the reader grasps the point, that privacy is the most essential attribute of any garden, whatever type or period."[16]

By 1920 Shipman had collaborated with Platt on at least ten projects for which supporting evidence remains and probably another twenty or so in the capacity of "silent partner."[17] Shipman's client list provides nineteen additional names who were also Platt clients: Vincent Astor, John Jay Chapman, George R. Dyer, Allen F. Edwards, Dr. John Elliot, David M. Goodrich, A. Conger Good-year, John Henry Hammond, Meredith Hare, Erskine B. Ingram, L. C. Ledyard, Arthur McGraw, William Gwinn Mather, Eugene Meyer, Richard D. Merrill,

Lake vista, The Moorings, Russell A. Alger estate, Grosse Pointe, Mich., 1917. Photo Thomas Ellison, 1930s. RMC-Cornell Univ. Library

Pool garden, Alger garden, 1917. Photo Thomas Ellison, 1930s. RMC-Cornell Univ. Library

R. D. Pruyn, Lansing F. Reed, W. Hinckle Smith, and Francis M. Weld. She would continue to work with him through the 1920s, although with less frequency (almost certainly in response to Platt's shrinking residential practice). The precise extent of their collaboration remains elusive. To one client Shipman later wrote, "For some years I did all of the gardens related to Charles Platt's houses." Another client claimed that Platt "would not build a house unless Ellen Shipman did the landscaping."[18] Neither statement was entirely accurate. Platt may have preferred to work with Shipman but, occasionally, he collaborated with other landscape architects, including the Olmsted Brothers. Neither was Shipman tied to Platt's practice; she would also work with many other architects during her active career—Roger H. Bullard, Clark and Arms, Delano and Aldrich, Alfred Hopkins, Harrie T. Lindeberg, Mott B. Schmidt, John F. Staub, and Horace Trumbauer, among others. But she would do some of her most interesting work on her own.

CHAPTER FOUR

A STYLE OF HER OWN

BETWEEN 1912 and 1919, Shipman's solo work progressed from cautious competence to highly personal expression. Pivotal collaborations with Platt sharpened her design sense, while they established a firm base for an expanding network of contacts and clients. Shipman mastered architectural skills, techniques for preparing engineering specifications, and the intricacies of large-scale planting schemes. She continued to struggle with spatial design, but from the first, she grasped the importance of an intimate relationship between house and garden, whereby the garden becomes a "shadow of the house." She relied on the same principles that had so often led Platt to success: axial layouts, careful proportional relationships between house and garden architecture, and strong visual and physical connections between house and garden. As did Platt, Shipman preferred to see house and garden develop as a single integrated unit. Her advice to one client, to "see me before you see your architect, or even buy the grounds," was likely repeated many times.[1]

In some respects, however, Shipman's gardens diverged sharply from those of her mentor. Whereas Platt's approach often called for radical regrading and replanting, Shipman explored the advantages of keeping to the original lay of the land: "Design as nearly as possible to the existing grades," she advised in the Garden Note Book.[2] Shipman's independent, early ideas about grading and architectural intervention are especially apparent in the small seaside garden she designed in 1912 for Samuel D. Warren, in Mattapoisset, Massachusetts. Defined on one side by a wall of evergreens, the garden consisted of beds of phlox and lilies and converging stone walks. A sundial and a Lutyens bench—at that time a novelty in America—appear to have been the design's two ornaments.

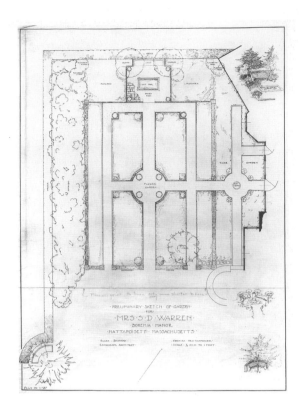

Preliminary sketch of Garden,
Bohemia Manor, Samuel D. Warren
estate, Mattapoisset, Mass., ink on
linen, 1912. RMC-Cornell Univ.
Library

Breezy, unstudied, romantic, the design incorporated several existing trees and
stopped at a distance from the shoreline, opening to a broad expanse of informal
lawn. Shipman was responding strongly to elements that preceded her involvement: the big trees, the flat grades, and, most significant, the summery, seaside
character of the site. It is likely that the narrow plant palette reflected a specific
request from the client, who may have been a collector.

The horticultural interests of her clients would play an enormous role in Shipman's work throughout her career. "When I am planning a garden," she wrote,
"I always feel that it should be according to the owner's desire," and, elsewhere,
"I feel strongly that each garden that I do is like a portrait of the person and
should express their likes and dislikes."[3] Shipman sometimes used plants she
actively disliked when a client specifically requested them—Colorado spruce
was one loathsome specimen that many of her customers seemed to covet. But
such acquiescence may not have enhanced Shipman's artistic recognizability.
Many of her colleagues were more inclined to argue with their clients' opinions if
disagreements came up. For instance, when a dispute erupted between Warren
Manning and William Mather (precisely over the use of spruce), Manning did
not yield to Mather but made it his duty to "educate" his client about the subtle-
ties of the native, deciduous palette he proposed instead.[4] Less flexible artistic
personalities, such as Manning's or Platt's, often appealed to prospective clients—

Fieldstone path, Warren garden, 1912. Photo Edith Hastings Tracy. RMC-Cornell Univ. Library

Warren garden, 1912. Photo Edith Hastings Tracy. RMC-Cornell Univ. Library

Warren garden three months after construction, 1912. Photo Shipman office. RMC-Cornell Univ. Library

especially to men, most of whom did not know a hosta from a horsechestnut. Shipman's more frequent contact with women clients, who were often extremely knowledgeable and informed gardeners themselves, probably helped to shape her collaborative design approach.

Shipman's March 1912 design for Alanson Daniels, on Boston's North Shore, harmonized with its country setting and a seventeenth-century house. Shipman's layout featured a Colonial Revival dooryard garden of hardy plants and, behind the house, the juxtaposition of a new design—a series of rectangular beds and walks culminating in a pool and semicircular "apse"—with an existing orchard. Thus the garden's character derived directly from its setting: the ancient orchard and its evocation of the larger agricultural landscape. By combining traditional New England landscape forms—such as the orchard and stone walls—with unexpectedly "modern," Jekyll-inspired plantings, Shipman's design signaled a move into new territory. This was one of the first instances where she used bold foliage—hosta, *Bergenia,* and iris—to strong sculptural effect. (Hosta quickly became a mainstay of Shipman's; she claimed she could not make a garden without it: "like the charity of the Bible—it covers the shortcomings of many other plants.")[5] The deliberateness with which the plants were arranged and the careful relationships resulting between them and the architectural elements was quietly revolutionary.

Although Shipman's planting experiments had transcended Cornish tradition, she remained true to the gardening fundamentals she had learned there. She continued to rely on her own experience, observing "under what conditions a plant

Old Farms, Alanson L. Daniels estate, Wenham, Mass., 1913. Photo Edith Hastings Tracy, 1914. RMC-Cornell Univ. Library

Sketch plan for walled garden,
Daniels garden, ink and wash
on paper, March 1913.
RMC- Cornell Univ. Library

Walled garden, Daniels garden, 1913. Photo Edith Hastings Tracy. RMC-Cornell Univ. Library

does best" and using this information to visualize it "in the picture." Like many designers, Shipman began each garden with a mental image. Once the plan had taken form and the inevitable design complications were resolved, it was realized in tangible materials: water, stone, wood, and plants. Shipman once commented that she used plants "as a painter uses the colors from his palette." Her recommendation to "eschew all outlandish plants" was an extension of this orientation.[6] Big horticultural budgets and competition among clients often led to collections of dwarf, oddly pigmented, weeping, and otherwise-altered horticultural wonders. But Shipman had no taste for oddities that would draw attention away from the larger picture and undermine her goal of a cohesive image.

THE PLAN

Ellen Shipman advised would-be garden makers to "remember that the design of your place is its skeleton upon which you will later plant to make your picture. Keep that skeleton as simple as possible."[7] Shipman's plan for the Dora Murdocks garden, likely a pre-professional effort, which she later identified as her first plan, shows the essence of the Platt-derived, axial approach from which she only occasionally deviated.[8] The herringbone-patterned brick paths, vine-covered garden walls, fruit tree standards, flanking perennial beds, and central fountain provided a generic working vocabulary for many future projects.

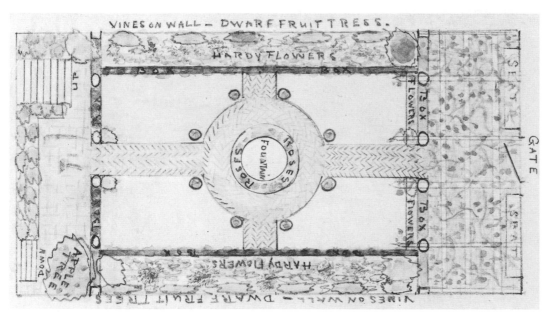

Plan for Dora Murdocks garden, Baltimore, Md. Nancy Angell Streeter Collection

A Style of Her Own   53

A country garden for Philip B. Jennings was typical of the basic spatial arrangement that guided Shipman's best solo work for the first decade of her practice. Detailed plans by Shipman's first assistant, Elizabeth Leonard Strang, with evocative thumbnail sketches penned in the borders, show the intended development of the Bennington, Vermont, project. Shipman designed two large rectangular gardens—one for flowers, one for vegetables—in axial alignment with the end of the house by Harrie T. Lindeberg, whom Shipman knew through Cornish connections.[9] An informal lawn bounded by screen plantings lay on the other side of the house. Later that year construction drawings were prepared; planting plans followed in 1915.

Access to the flower garden was across a house terrace and down a flight of steps. The area was structured by a series of brick-paved walks that broke the rectangle into eight beds. A fountain basin marked the central intersection. The two walks continued beyond the walled formal garden into the adjoining, much larger (160 by 100–foot) vegetable garden, where they terminated in a semicircular loop at the far end. There a small, apse-shaped space was set aside for annuals. The major circulation pattern of the two-part garden was, in other words, a long rectangle. The starkness of the plan would scarcely have been obvious to visitors distracted by the charms of the diminutive teahouse, dovecote (soon to become a

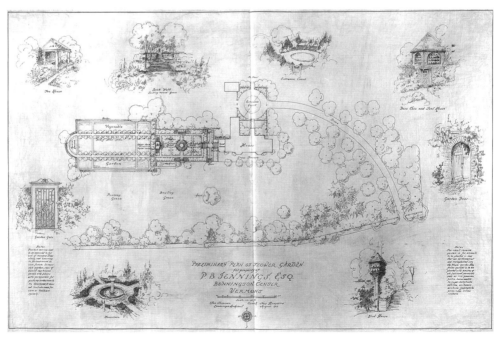

Preliminary plan of flower garden, Philip B. Jennings estate, Bennington, Vt., ink on linen, August 1914. RMC-Cornell Univ. Library

The Gardens of Ellen Biddle Shipman

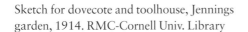
Dove Cote and Tool House

Garden Gate

Sketch for dovecote and toolhouse, Jennings garden, 1914. RMC-Cornell Univ. Library

Sketch for gate, Jennings garden, 1914. RMC-Cornell Univ. Library

trademark of many Shipman gardens), two-story birdhouse, and Chippendale-style gate. Shipman also noted masses of "iris, paeonies, funkia, hemerocallis, larkspur, hollyhocks, achillea, anthemis, anchusa, gypsophila, primroses, lilies, rockets" that would have made the picture considerably more luxurious than the plan's skeletal geometry suggests. The scheme captured Shipman's basic approach: keep the plan simple—almost always rectangular, in axial relation to the house—and make it interesting with plants and garden architecture.

The distinctive style of the Jennings presentation drawing developed by Elizabeth Leonard Strang quickly became the preferred visual vehicle of the Shipman office. And long after Strang had left Shipman's employ, the style was continued by others.[10] Though the concept was not entirely original, these drawings differed subtly from those of other offices in at least two respects: schematic layout and graphic style. Some practitioners combined plans with architectural or planting vignettes, but it was more common for these elements to be drawn separately. In Shipman's office, presentation drawings routinely combined plans with charming pen-and-ink illustrations that figuratively took viewers on a walk through the garden. These images struck a more informal note than did Beatrix Farrand's ethereal axiometric watercolors, for example, or Fletcher Steele's office's highly detailed pencil sketches. Their resemblance to period book illustrations is strong evidence for the theory that Shipman was gaining much of her design information from printed sources. The graphic style is similar to Inigo Triggs's *Formal Gardens in England and Scotland,* a large folio with plans and thumbnail sketches of architectural features, and to illustrations in Thomas

A Style of Her Own   55

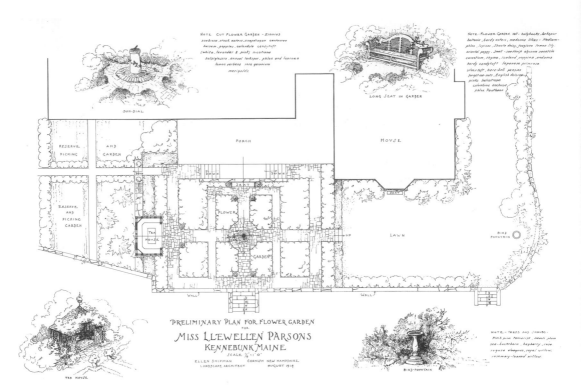

Preliminary plan for flower garden, Llewellyn Parsons estate, Kennebunk, Me., ink on linen, August 1914. RMC-Cornell Univ. Library

Mawson's *Art and Craft of Garden Making.* The sketches also resemble the renderings and perspective drawings of country houses found in *American Architect and Building News.*

Shipman's elaborate plans also carried horticultural instructions, written in meticulous, though personal, language, almost as a letter to the client. Her instructions on the Jennings plan are typical: "The small reserve garden is for annuals to be planted in rows that can be thinned out and transplanted into the flower garden…. In the vegetable garden, rows of dwarf apple, crab, peach and plums with perennials for picking underneath. As designed it does not include room for corn or hubbard squash."

In 1914, Strang drew the plan for the Llewellyn Parsons commission, a flower garden on axis with a large porch overlooking the ocean view. (The axis is indicated by a short black line.) Visitors entered the garden by descending either of two short flights of steps. Brick walkways divided the rectangular area into eight beds. The small teahouse (rendered in the plan's lower left-hand corner) provided a stop to the long axis. The strong similarities apparent between this and the Jennings plan, also dated 1914, reveal a decidedly "Shipmanesque" style emerging in both garden and graphic design.

The Gardens of Ellen Biddle Shipman

Few of the circumstances of these early commissions are known. Shipman was called in to design the Parsons landscape four years after the Olmsted Brothers firm had subdivided the extensive Kennebunk family compound. Arthur Shurcliff, who was with the Olmsteds at the time of the original work, knew Ellen Shipman from their Harvard-Radcliffe days and may have recommended her for the job. Shurcliff returned to work on the landscape in 1931, long after he had left the Olmsted firm. Shipman also returned, sometime after that date, to add to plantings along the entry drive and develop a garden of native plants.[11] (Parsons was an energetic though somewhat restless client—she hired Fletcher Steele for further garden developments in 1945.)

More spatially complex—and sensually rich—than any of these early projects was the garden at Grahampton, the Henry Croft estate in Greenwich, Connecticut. A grading plan and site and planting plans confirm Shipman's involvement beginning in 1917. The intricacy of the design may have been prompted by unusual circumstances of site rather than any particular desire on Shipman's part to experiment. Her task seems to have been to develop new gardens beyond those already in place. The original design, by James Leal Greenleaf, had been carefully conceived to form an integrated whole.[12] Shipman elected to give three new areas, none of which was visible from the earlier garden, a diminutive scale

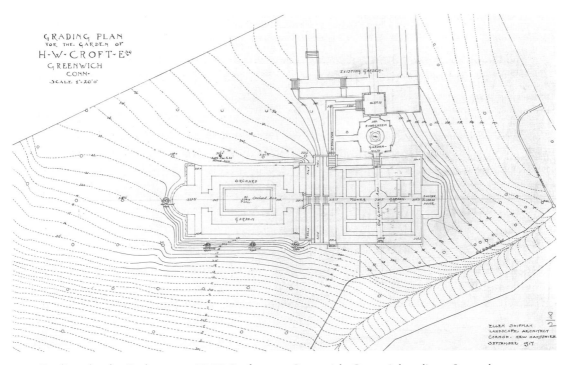

Grading plan for Grahampton, H. W. Croft estate, Greenwich, Conn., ink on linen, September 1917. RMC-Cornell Univ. Library

A Style of Her Own   57

Croft garden, 1917. Photo Mattie Edwards Hewitt, c. 1922. RMC-Cornell Univ. Library

and a sense of enclosure. An evergreen garden, a flower garden, and a pool garden were attached in an L shape. The fourteen-foot drop in elevation allowed Shipman to set up plunging and rising views across the two main axes. One of these views led to a sculpture of Diana, added in 1927.

The new area was planted so that the three gardens were not all visible from any single vantage point. This sense of mystery was heightened by the garden's seclusion, as though the outside world, including the rest of the property, had ceased to exist. Shipman held an unswerving belief in the importance of privacy: "Planting, however beautiful, is not a garden. A garden must be enclosed … or otherwise it would merely be a cultivated area."[13] In this she differed somewhat from Platt, who tended to utilize walls and hedges to establish spatial separation but one that rarely offered the sense of seclusion possible with tall walls of foliage. "Some gardens, like some homes, afford little more privacy than a shop window. Better one room that is your own," Shipman advised, "than a whole house exposed to the world, better a tiny plot where you can be alone than a great expanse without this essential attribute of the real garden."[14]

Pond, Croft garden, 1917. Photo Mattie Edwards Hewitt, c. 1922. RMC-Cornell Univ. Library

Vista to *Diana* added in 1927, Croft garden. Photo Mattie Edwards Hewitt, c. 1928. RMC-Cornell Univ. Library

Stone bench, Croft garden, 1917. Photo Mattie Edwards
Hewitt, c. 1922. RMC-Cornell Univ. Library

In her first plan for Philip Gossler's estate in New Canaan, Connecticut, Shipman experimented, unsuccessfully, with a complex spatial organization that transcended any of her earlier designs. The initial 1919 design exhibited an extensive and somewhat arbitrary arrangement of individual garden rooms, whose proportions bore little relation to the house. Although the placement of these rooms was determined by existing trees and shrubs (and therefore may have been more convincing in elevation than in plan), the number and size of the areas would have overwhelmed the rather modest house. A large budget and her client's prominence—Gossler was director of the board of Guaranty Trust—apparently intimidated Shipman into trying something beyond her still-developing capabilities. But the failure may have guided her back to her early principles and strengthened her adherence to them in the process. On her second try, Shipman produced a less ambitious and quite successful design. Years later, a *House Beautiful* critic noted that "nothing seems to equal the enclosed garden in friendliness."[15] Gossler was obviously pleased, too; when he moved to Long Island in 1925, he commissioned a new garden from Shipman there.

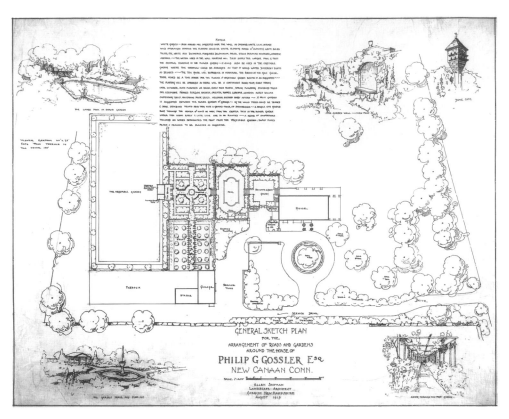

General sketch plan for Philip G. Gossler estate, New Canaan, Conn., ink on linen, August 1919. RMC-Cornell Univ. Library

THE PLANTING

Shipman also actively experimented with planting design during her first decade of practice. Three examples from the late 1910s show the range of her inquiry. At Wampus, the John Magee estate in Mount Kisco, New York, Shipman balanced an unconventional scheme of architectural elements—one of her most developed to date—with a particularly rich combination of plants.[16] Comparison with Shipman's designs for Platt's gardens, at the Alger or Starr estates, for example, suggests that she may have been inspired to greater originality when she had complete control of a project. When Shipman was commissioned to design the architectural and spatial frameworks and the plantings, her imagination could tackle both simultaneously. It was a far more complicated charge than simply enlivening a preexisting frame.

At Wampus, Shipman's intricately detailed brick walks, terraces, and pergola were an unexpected mixture of Italian, British, and traditional American motifs.

Terrace overlooking Hudson River, Wampus, John Magee estate, Mount Kisco, N.Y., c. 1918.
Photo Mattie Edwards Hewitt, c. 1918. RMC-Cornell Univ. Library

Pergola, Magee garden, 1916. Photo Mattie Edwards Hewitt, c. 1918. RMC-Cornell Univ. Library

Pergola and fountain terrace, Magee garden, 1916. Photo Mattie Edwards Hewitt, c. 1918. RMC-Cornell Univ. Library

Slender Corinthian columns supported a wood trellis that cast intricate shadows on the herringbone brick terrace beneath. Antique urns, tank, and benches stood next to cast concrete ornaments that recalled classical prototypes. Shipman's lyrical plantings served to emphasize the architecture rather than counterbalance it. Mattie Edwards Hewitt's photographs from 1923 show a mature garden awash with June-blooming plants. Shipman's wisteria-covered pergola bordered a small, hedged enclosure and a riot of cottage garden flowers. Dense clumps of rhododendron and green shrubbery on an adjacent terrace were reflected in a small pool and provided a lustrous green counterfoil.

The same year, 1916, Shipman began a summer garden for Julia Fish in Greenport, Long Island, as strikingly simple as Wampus was complex. The garden's main feature was double perennial borders, nearly four hundred feet in length, set against a backdrop of cedars and shrubbery. The color-graded borders ranged from lavender to pink to blue on one side, from blue to white on the other. A wide turf path separated the beds, as was common in British gardens of the period. Shipman kept the defining walls and floor of the area green; the one slight change in elevation was negotiated by inconspicuous turf steps. The centerpiece, a small reflecting pool, made the garden sparkle from every side. Each view across it terminated in a different focal point: sculpture, a bench, a garden house. Rare construction photographs, of about 1916, reveal the extent to which the garden was pure invention. Mattie Hewitt's photographs, taken ten years later, belie the bleakness of the open field which confronted Shipman on her first visit to the site.

Shipman's initial inspiration for the design may have come from Gertrude Jekyll's *Colour Schemes for the Flower Garden,* a copy of which was in her private library.[17] The book detailed Jekyll's pioneering efforts in blending colors and contrasting textures so as to evoke the billowing effect of an Impressionist painting. This concept, as well as suggestions for single-color borders, inspired many amateur and professional gardeners, but few if any had the horticultural mastery to realize Jekyll's ideas. Shipman's borders for the Fish garden were spectacular, but in fact were atypical in her oeuvre. Most of her later color borders—such as the one at Stan Hywet Hall in Akron, Ohio—juxtaposed jewellike colors to create a stained-glass-window effect rather than an impressionistic wash.

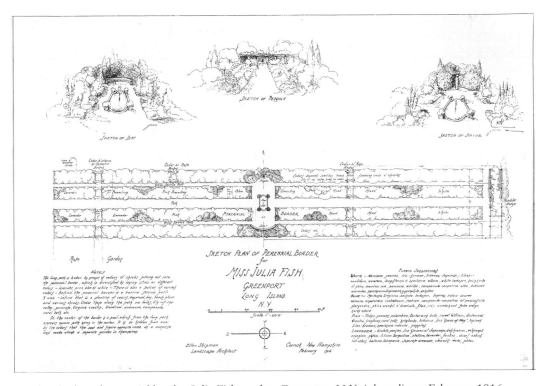

Sketch plan of perennial border, Julia Fish garden, Greenport, N.Y., ink on linen, February 1916. RMC-Cornell Univ. Library

Perennial borders, Fish garden, 1916. Photo Mattie Edwards Hewitt, August 1927. RMC-Cornell Univ. Library

Pool and borders, Fish garden, 1916. Photo Mattie Edwards Hewitt, August 1927. RMC-Cornell Univ. Library

Fish garden under construction, 1916. Photo Shipman office, c. 1916. RMC-Cornell Univ. Library

Pool, Fish garden, 1916. Photo Mattie Edwards Hewitt, August 1927.
RMC-Cornell Univ. Library

Shipman's planting skills reached an early apogee in her 1919 garden in Easthampton, Long Island, for Mary and Neltje Pruyn, who were artists and volun-
teer social workers. The referral undoubtedly came from Platt, who had recently
remodeled the modest cottage. Fletcher Steele wrote appreciatively of his colleague's design: "Part of the unusually successful Colonial feeling here is due to
the fact that stiff accuracy has been avoided. Note even that one side of the path
is edged with brick—the other with a board."[18] As Shipman's confidence grew,
her handling of plants and materials became more relaxed and intuitive. The
inspiration for the tiny garden was Colonial Revival, but Shipman eschewed the
traditional dooryard garden's haphazard mix of color and bloom in favor of
more sophisticated plant combinations. Comparison with Stephen Parrish's
Northcote sheds light on the artistry of Shipman's plant choices.

The Gardens of Ellen Biddle Shipman

Mary and Neltje Pruyn garden, 1920, East Hampton, N.Y. Photo Mattie Edwards Hewitt, c. 1923. RMC-Cornell Univ. Library

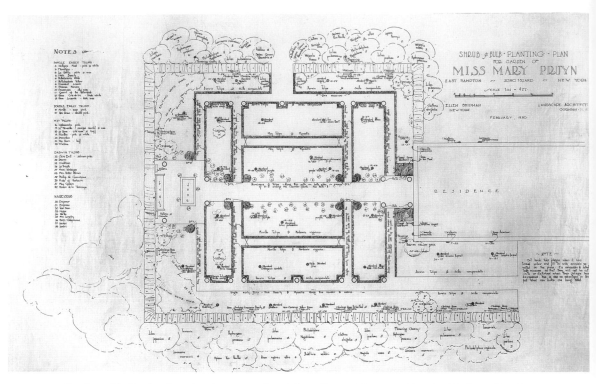

Shrub and bulb planting plan, Pruyn garden, ink on linen, February 1920. RMC-Cornell Univ. Library

At Northcote, the general impression of abundant, healthy bloom and unstudied, horticultural confusion bespoke the care of a dedicated amateur and from this derived its sense of joy and naïveté. Each robust perennial clump maintained its identity as an individual block. Shipman, by contrast, arranged abstract drifts of plants of varying sizes, in varying shapes, in response to each plant's character and habit. Edges disappeared. Symmetry was avoided in favor of unexpected pairings and contrast. Bold-foliaged plants, such as peonies and anchusa, abutted ephemeral clouds of baby's breath and astilbe. Iris swords penetrated the less insistent, deeply lobed foliage of delphinium. Everywhere that the eye rested new combinations were revealed. The prim layout and profligate planting could scarcely have sounded two more different stylistic notes; in combination, they created something quite new.

CHAPTER FIVE

THE NEW YORK OFFICE

IN 1920, ELLEN decided to move her business to New York City. She may have been encouraged by the success of her brother Nicholas, who ran a successful law office there. (Biddle was the trustee for the Astor Estate Office, commercial clients of Charles Platt; Vincent Astor was a client of Ellen's.) The failure of her marriage, which ended in divorce in 1927, may also have provided her strong emotional as well as financial motivations to move. Shipman probably anticipated that her business would function much more efficiently from New York than from rural New Hampshire, particularly given the complexities of train travel. Additionally, Ellen's youngest child, Mary, had just turned twelve—old enough, in her mother's view, to attend boarding school.[1]

After considering other properties, Shipman bought a townhouse on Beekman Place, at the corner of East 50th Street. Sited on a high bluff overlooking the East River, the street had once looked down on slaughterhouses, but she saw great possibilities in the view and the location. The house was one of several older brick buildings that had recently been purchased by writers and actors who hoped to transform the former working-class neighborhood into a private enclave. By 1932, when William Bottomley's River House and its private landing were constructed, Beekman Place had become one of the city's most desirable addresses. Shipman later noted, "There is not in all New York another piece of property like it, for it has seclusion ... southern exposure, beauty of architecture, combined with the extended view of the East River."[2]

Shipman engaged architects Butler and Corse to assist her in remodeling the house. (A few years earlier, Charles Platt had drawn up renovation plans for another property, but they were not realized.) She wrestled with the challenge of

19–21 Beekman Place, New York, N.Y.
Photo Samuel H. Gottscho, c. 1927.
Nancy Angell Streeter Collection

creating separate quarters for the office, her residence, and two apartments on the upper floors. Shipman's ability to integrate interior design with architecture served her well here and proved to be an asset in later years, when she generated more income from interior work than from landscape design.

The renovations put the office door on Beekman Place and the entrance to Shipman's private quarters on the East 50th Street side. Photographs in a 1927 *House Beautiful* article record English Georgian furniture, a collection of Lowestoft china, decorative paneling, carvings, and wallcoverings from Chinese screens. Childe Hassam's view of Gloucester, a pastoral landscape by Willard Metcalf, and drawings by Maxfield Parrish brought reminders of the Cornish colony to New York. A bay window created the setting for a small shelf garden. Work quarters included a large drafting room and Shipman's private office, which overlooked the river. The walls of the reception room held photographs of the Fahnestock, Starr, Morris, and Cooper commissions. Copies of *House Beautiful, Historic Gardens of Virginia* (1923), and other publications, many of which undoubtedly contained images of Shipman's gardens, were spread on the table for waiting clients.[3]

Shipman's would prove to be one of the most durable of several New York offices run by women landscape architects.[4] Increasing publicity, the photogenic quality of her gardens, strong relations with garden club networks (particularly

The Gardens of Ellen Biddle Shipman

Dining room with Chinese screens used as wallpaper, Beekman Place. Photo Samuel H. Gottscho, c. 1927. Nancy Angell Streeter Collection

Bay window, Beekman Place. Photo Samuel H. Gottscho, c. 1927. Nancy Angell Streeter Collection

Office reception room, Beekman Place. Photo Samuel H. Gottscho, c. 1927. Nancy Angell Streeter Collection

the Garden Club of America), and Shipman's congeniality as a speaker, house-guest, and artist attracted scores of clients as the widespread demand for country houses kept the pool of prospective customers full. Shipman built up geographic networks of clients, often returning to do jobs for other family members, neighbors, and friends of an initial contact. She worked for twenty-four clients in Greenwich, Connecticut, seventeen in Mount Kisco, New York, and fifty-seven on Long Island. Other areas with significant client clusters were Houston, Buffalo, and Winston-Salem, North Carolina. In Grosse Pointe Shores, Michigan, she completed forty-four projects. In Ohio she had forty-five commissions, mostly estates outside Cleveland and Toledo.

Like Beatrix Farrand, Shipman employed women exclusively, relying heavily on graduates from the Lowthorpe School because she thought the training there "unsurpassed."[5] No documents reveal the basis for her policy, but at least two different circumstances could explain it. Certainly Shipman wanted to give women opportunities for training and jobs not otherwise available in a male-dominated field. She once wrote, "There is no profession so suited to [women], so needed and so repaying in every way—nor any that at once gives so much of health, wealth and happiness."[6] It is also likely that male applicants for positions in female landscape architectural practices were scarce.

By the late 1920s, Shipman's staff comprised up to five draftsmen, with as many as ten working on a temporary basis, and two secretaries.[7] Drainage and grading work were almost always subcontracted to engineering consultants. Among Shipman's most important assistants besides Elizabeth Leonard Strang were her designer and office manager, Louise Payson, who, like Strang, initially worked in Cornish, and draftsman Eleanor Hills Christie. Dorothy May Anderson and Mary P. Cunningham also worked for Shipman, as did Agnes Selkirk Clark. Clark and Edith Schryver became two of the best-known landscape architects trained in the office. Schryver was an excellent draftsman and worked on many important jobs in both the Cornish and the New York office until 1929, when she opened her own practice in partnership with Elizabeth Lord in Salem, Oregon.[8] Agnes Selkirk Clark's husband, Cameron Clark, was associated with the architectural firm of Clark and Arms, which worked with Shipman on several

Ellen Shipman in her Beekman Place office, New York, N.Y. Photo Bradley Studio, 1920s. Nancy Angell Streeter Collection

commissions, including the Philip Gossler residence in New Canaan, Connecticut, in 1919.

One assistant who did not go on to open her own office was Frances McCormic, a longtime associate of Shipman's and a close personal friend of her family. Shipman had quickly offered McCormic a job after she won a prize for model making at Lowthorpe in 1926; McCormic abandoned her formal studies and went to work for Shipman full-time. For two decades she was Shipman's office head, chief draftsman, and modelmaker. When she left in 1945 to take a job with Condé Nast, Shipman was slow to forgive her.[9]

Shipman's office procedures were conventional, although her involvement in every stage of development was not characteristic of the largest practices of the period, where principals were forced to assume more administrative roles. Each job began with a site visit and consultation. "I never have done and never expect to do a piece of work without seeing the place and making the plans especially for it," Shipman wrote to a client who had recklessly suggested that one of her plans for another project would do.[10] Initial visits were recorded in copious notes and photographs. These, along with a survey plan, rough sketches, and her broad recommendations, would be forwarded to her office with instructions for several alternative design solutions. Eleanor Christie recalled that upon receiving rough sketches that were often not drawn to scale, she and other assistants would work to "make it fit together." Several schemes would then be fleshed out for presentation to the client. For larger estates, a watercolor design was prepared. Only after the concept was approved and detailed construction drawings under way were planting plans drawn up. Shipman relied on her draftsmen to generate finished drawings and in some cases to supervise installation. While the staff worked out the details, she gave the final approvals.[11] Office correspondence from before the mid-1940s is sparse, so little information is available about the fees Shipman charged for her work. According to an invoice for a job in 1946, however, her fee was one hundred dollars, plus travel, for a consultation, and from twenty-five to one hundred dollars each for construction and planting plans.[12] As her workload increased, Shipman juggled numerous jobs simultaneously, spending much time traveling between distant geographic areas. For longer journeys she traveled by overnight train (always on a lower berth) and in later years by plane.

Most of Shipman's clients eventually became her personal friends. As did Platt, she often stayed in their homes rather than in hotels. She ate with the family and was entertained lavishly at luncheons where friends and neighbors—all of them prospective clients—could tap her for garden-making advice.[13] Not all practitioners were so inclined. Warren Manning and Beatrix Farrand, for example, enjoyed hotels and the respite they offered from round-the-clock socializing.

Shipman had her limits, too; she made it clear that cats were not welcome in her quarters and that she required a one-hour nap after lunch.[14]

According to one employee, Shipman "took endless trouble to see that her clients had all the information needed to execute her plans successfully."[15] Most plans included copious horticultural notes that explained what, how, and when to plant, how to stake, and what to replace the plant with when it started to fade. The instructions penned into the margins of her plan for the superintendent's gardens at the U.S. Military Academy at West Point were typical in their specificity and rigor:

> STAKING—After the preparation of the soil and the planting, the next most important thing for the success of the garden is proper staking. This should be attended to most diligently, as most plants, if not staked from the beginning, form roots on their stems and spread out, leaving no room for less hardy and less vigorous adjacent plants. Small stakes should be used at first and replaced with larger ones as the plants increase in size. The plants must not be tied to the stakes. The stakes should be placed around the plant or group of one variety and raffia tied to the stakes, leaving the plant or plants free in the center. Asters, chrysanthemums, and other large plants can be trained or staked carefully about September first, to lean forward and cover any vacant place where plants have died down.

Shipman's horticultural standards were exacting and her tolerance of inferior work extremely limited. She advised on seasonal maintenance, making once- or twice-yearly visits to her gardens to monitor their condition. This procedure was not unusual—most of the era's other designers also suggested it to their clients. Less common was Shipman's practice of administering an annual discretionary sum to purchase plants. A request from her to a client for one such arrangement began, rather exasperatedly, "quite frequently you are away and the time for planting then goes by, and we sometimes lose a whole year."[16]

Shipman's recommendations about regular visits may have been less insistent when women gardeners or caretakers were involved. In a letter to William and Elizabeth Mather, her Cleveland clients at Gwinn (ironically, one of the few estates that ever employed a female superintendent), Shipman stated, "I never secure men for any place unless I see it at least twice a year, because I have never found any man who is able to keep a garden or place in the condition that I thought it should be unless I supervise it twice a year."[17] Shipman's British contemporary Viscountess Wolseley confessed a similar prejudice to her students at the Glynde School for Landscape Gardening in Sussex: "We want to banish once and for all the inferior, rule-of-thumb, slow-thinking, inartistic man-gardener whom we have tolerated for so long and in his place require intelligent, educated ladies, who will direct and supervise as ably and in some cases even better than the very best type of male gardener."[18]

Despite Shipman's advice to her clients, her own gardener at Brook Place was male. John Hathaway, an Englishman, also served as Shipman's superintendent on an important commission for Samuel Salvage during the late 1920s. He later went to work for Shipman's clients the Ormsby Mitchells in Greenwich, Connecticut, and then the Ralph Haneses, in Winston-Salem, at which time Charles Meyette took over Hathaway's duties at Brook Place. Shipman enjoyed a warmly satisfying relationship with both Meyette and his wife, and remembered her caretaker handsomely in her will.[19]

Each summer until World War II, Shipman removed her practice to New Hampshire, where work continued at a more leisurely pace. Frances McCormic, who spent many summers at Brook Place, remembered the annual packing of the office paraphernalia and moving to the country as a "big production"—and not one of her own choosing, since she found little to do in the country when she was not working. McCormic lived in an apartment above the garage at Brook Place, while the other employees boarded elsewhere.[20] The seasonal move, in addition to the taxing travel associated with the job, would have made it difficult for an employee to maintain a marriage or family responsibilities. It is not surprising, then, that many of Shipman's were single and childless.

In Cornish, Shipman entertained lavishly, with the help of four servants and the cook she brought from New York. She continued as an active member of the Mothers' and Daughters' Club in Plainfield, where she gave slide-illustrated lectures. She also held annual competitions for the colony's most artistically designed garden, the prize a twenty-dollar gold piece.[21] During these years, her daughter Mary became an accomplished equestrian. Evan also developed an interest in horses, but preferred to watch them race. By 1925, he was routinely spending summers at Brook Place and wintering in Paris, where he wrote poetry and befriended several writers, including Ernest Hemingway.[22]

During the 1920s, the gardens at Brook Place were in their prime. The moment recorded by Mattie Edwards Hewitt in 1923 and featured in *House and Garden* the following year shows a country landscape of great charm.[23] A brick terrace laid in a basketweave pattern kept tune with the traditional New England farmhouse and the millstone at the doorstep. Old wooden buckets filled with conical hemlocks performed the same decorative role as Charles Platt's bay trees had in his gardens, but in a country vernacular. The brick-paved terrace continued around to the covered porch alongside the pergola, where the tea table was set on another millstone. The vine-covered porch, seen from the middle of the garden, was cloaked to provide a shady retreat. A small

Brick-paved terrace, Brook Place, Plainfield, N.H. Photo Mattie Edwards Hewitt, 1923. Nancy Angell Streeter Collection

pool, closely modeled on one designed for a client, provided a flicker of reflected light.

Phlox, peonies, delphiniums, and other hardy perennials filled the big beds, just as in Shipman's design for the Pruyn garden; dianthus and hardy geranium bordered plank-lined dirt paths. The billowing perennials were bolstered by hemlock cubes topped by topiaried globes. At the far end of the garden, a low stone wall separated the private compound from the road. Birch and other trees tied the garden to the outer landscape. Two large vegetable gardens kept the larders full, and a cutting garden supplied fresh flowers for the house. One year's autumn seed order included calendula, candytuft, alyssum, *Centaurea Americana*, delphiniums, and mixed Shirley poppies.[24] At Brook Place, Shipman was both designer and dirt gardener. The garden's mix of sophistication and unpretentiousness resonated with her own.

Loggia, Brook Place. Photo Mattie Edwards Hewitt, 1923. Plainfield Historical Society

View through garden, Brook Place. Photo Mattie Edwards Hewitt, 1923. Nancy Angell Streeter Collection

Stone wall and plantings, Brook Place. Photo Mattie Edwards Hewitt, 1923. Nancy Angell Streeter Collection

CHAPTER SIX

ARTISTIC MATURITY

SHIPMAN'S CLIENT roster was rapidly growing thanks to publicity in popular magazines and books. Gardens planted during the previous decade were reaching their peak by the early 1920s when images by Mattie Edwards Hewitt, Jessie Tarbox Beals, Frances Benjamin Johnston, and other superb photographers were published with articles about Shipman's work. Beginning in 1921, a flood of photo essays chronicling her gardens appeared in *The Garden, House and Garden,* and *House Beautiful,* as well as in professional journals showing collaborative work with architects. By 1924, for instance, the Magee garden of 1916 had been featured in all three popular magazines, in Elsa Rehmann's book *Garden-Making,* and in the 1923 annual exhibition of the Architectural League of New York.[1]

The rapidity with which Shipman's fame spread during the early 1920s is staggering. Many new commissions resulted from word-of-mouth recommendations; in addition, news of her abilities was circulated by organizations such as the Garden Club of America, whose members became clients. Noticeably absent from Shipman's growing list of clients, however, were referrals traceable to her family, where they might normally be expected to have originated.

Shipman's gardens from the 1920s were ever more assured and varied in style, according to the requirements of site, client, and budget. Often the new designs incorporated traditional architectural motifs illustrated in Shipman's library; her collection included as many books on architecture and interiors as on horticulture.[2] Large folios depicting Majorcan houses, English cottages, and French provincial architecture and several on English Georgian architecture and interiors provided a wealth of detail. She also owned several British reference

Samuel Morris garden, Chestnut Hill, Pa., 1922. Photo Mattie Edwards Hewitt, c. 1924. RMC-Cornell Univ. Library

books on garden architecture: Jekyll and Lawrence Weaver's *Gardens for Small Country Houses* (1912), Weaver's *Small Country Houses* (1914), and Jekyll and Christopher Hussey's *Garden Ornament* (1927). These titles presented a strong visual case for a vernacular Arts and Crafts approach to design, as opposed to the formal Beaux Arts philosophy promoted in American books at the time. Two other influential books by the English architect H. Inigo Triggs, *The Art of Garden Design in Italy* (1906) and *Garden Craft in Europe* (1913), allowed Shipman to examine in detail historical examples of garden design. Fletcher Steele's *Design in the Little Garden* (1924) and Wilhelm Miller's *What England Can Teach Us about Gardening* (1911) were among the few representations of works by American landscape architects. Standard horticultural reference works by Taylor and Liberty Hyde Bailey as well as monographs on lilies, roses, and clematis stood alongside volumes of garden writing by Neltje Blanchan, Helena Rutherfurd Ely, and Louise Beebe Wilder. Shipman also owned several titles by Louisa Yeomans King and Mabel Cabot Sedgwick's practical book *The Garden Month by Month* (1907); both writers were also clients.

The Gardens of Ellen Biddle Shipman

Three of Shipman's largest commissions from the 1920s—for Carll Tucker, Samuel Salvage, and Ormsby Mitchell—came to her near the end of the decade, when her design powers were at their height. But modest jobs were more common, circumscribed by budget, site size, or preexisting designs by other landscape architects. Shipman's availability to work up an elaborate planting scheme for a few hundred dollars proved irresistible to dozens of clients whose resources were limited or who already owned grand gardens that simply needed to have their plantings rejuvenated. These smaller jobs usually involved new plantings and designs for pools, terraces, flights of steps, and other architectural features; most did not include site design or extensive grading.

Typical was the commission for the Windsor Whites in Chagrin Falls, Ohio, a village outside Cleveland where Shipman would eventually complete a dozen

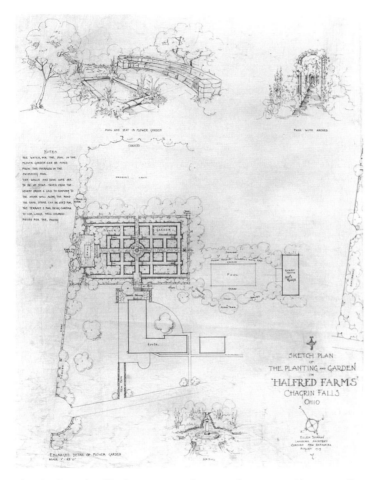

Sketch plan of Halfred Farms, Windsor T. White estate, Chagrin Falls, Ohio, ink on linen, August 1919. RMC-Cornell Univ. Library

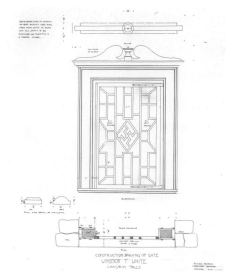

Construction drawing of gate,
White garden, ink on trace,
April 1919. RMC-Cornell Univ.
Library

View through beds, White garden, 1919. Photo Tebbs and Knell, 1920s. RMC-Cornell Univ.
Library

White garden under construction. Photo Shipman office, 7 May 1922. RMC-Cornell Univ.
Library

jobs. The Halfred Farms project began in 1919 while Shipman was still in the
Cornish office, but construction and planting continued through the early 1920s.
Warren Manning, whose professional path crossed frequently with Shipman's,
also began working for the Whites that year. It may have been their first of many
professional intersections.[3] Manning oversaw the layout of the general plan,
which necessarily included existing features—such as the 1860 farmhouse. Shipman was asked to supply a design specifically for a formal garden. Certainly, the
two would have communicated with each other about ongoing development.

In Shipman's plan, a large rectangular lawn stretched beside the farmhouse
on a lower terrace reached by a flight of flagstone steps. Directly opposite the
steps was a Chippendale-style gate, a formal answer to the guest house designed
by Bryant Fleming, which was probably part of the Manning plan. Manning
was not particularly adept at garden architecture; one wonders, however, why
the guest house was not part of Shipman's design responsibilities. It may have
pre-dated her involvement. At the foot of the garden were a semicircular stone
terrace and small rectangular pool. Large square beds of perennials, flowering

Pool, White garden, 1919. Photo Parade Studio, 1920s. RMC-Cornell Univ. Library

shrubs, arborvitae, and rose arches filled the central garden space with a jumble of color and fragrance. Around the pool, unexpected contrast erupted between the formal juniper spires that recalled the upright forms of Italian cypress and the naturalistic treatment of the plantings that merged into surrounding woods. The untamed aspect of this planting may have reflected the subtle influence of

The Gardens of Ellen Biddle Shipman

Manning, whose informal tastes had undoubtedly imbued the overall design with a relaxed spirit. Alongside the square garden, delineated by a low stone wall, was a rectangular iris garden with a small oval pool at its center. The ornamental garden areas nestled closely to house; through the small complex of farm outbuildings, winding roads led to apple orchards and meadows filled with bobolinks.

Shipman developed a close friendship with the Whites, who helped her career by recommending her services to friends and relatives and, years later, donated money to a scholarship fund Shipman oversaw for the Lowthorpe School. In 1942, she thanked them for making Cleveland "one of the bright spots" of her professional career. (The Cleveland area was also unusually rich in Shipman trainees, many of whom had flourishing practices.) According to one source, Shipman met Charles Lindbergh during one of her many stays at Halfred Farms and caught a plane ride home with him to New York.[4]

Shipman's charge for the Robert S. Brewster estate, Avalon, in Mount Kisco, New York, was also characteristic of her more modest jobs. Avalon's extensive

Pool vista, Avalon, Robert S. Brewster Jr. estate, Mount Kisco, N.Y., early 1920s. Photo Mattie Edwards Hewitt, c. 1923. RMC-Cornell Univ. Library

Arch and plantings, Brewster garden, early 1920s. Photo Mattie Edwards Hewitt, c. 1923. RMC-Cornell Univ. Library

grounds had been originally designed by Charles Delano of Delano and Aldrich in 1912 according to Beaux Arts principals of spatial layout, yet much of the surrounding woodland had been left intact.[5] Shipman was hired in the early 1920s, probably in response to aging or otherwise unsatisfactory plantings, to redesign the central, ornamental part of the scheme. The original planting designer is not known; Delano, an architect, was probably not much involved on a horticultural level.

In Delano's design, a sunken garden and pool were revealed to visitors as they emerged from beneath a circular pergola to descend a wide flight of steps onto the garden's "carpet," a broad stretch of lawn surrounded on three sides by dense woods. The oval pool provided Shipman a setting for what was, essentially, a border wrapped around its perimeter. June photographs record iris, lilies, dianthus, hosta, and Wichuraiana rose spilling into the water. The delicate texture of Shipman's border was repeated on a bolder scale by flanking beds that mimicked the pool's curve.

Pergola, Brewster garden, early 1920s. Photo Mattie Edwards Hewitt, c. 1923. RMC-Cornell Univ. Library

Artistic Maturity   93

Shipman told one interviewer that she used no more than six to eight main flowering plants in each design and "let each, in its season, dominate the garden. For the time one flower is the guest of honor and is merely supplemented with other flowers." There were exceptions to this approach, of course, but Shipman used it to guide most of her planting decisions. The strategy had several practical implications. First, because there were fewer numbers of varieties in bloom at any one time, color harmonies were less complex and therefore easier to control. It was also possible to achieve a more distinctive overall impression. In Shipman's view, a well-placed grouping of flowers against a green background produced a more dramatic effect than unrelieved blocks of color did; she had discovered that green shrubbery was useful for "lending lights and shadows" to bloom, increasing their impact and beauty. Last, because only a small number of flowers burst into bloom at any given moment, Shipman could spread out the show and thereby achieve a longer season of color.[6]

The wisteria-draped pergola at Avalon offered a different sort of planting opportunity altogether: two cascades of white Wichuraiana rose cushioned the curving stairs, emphasizing the delicate proportions of the steps. A mixed scheme, such as that surrounding the pool, would have undermined the delicacy and focused simplicity of the picture. Few of Shipman's step plantings achieved this level of drama, however. Most often her steps involved minor changes in level and gradual transitions from one garden area to the next. Materials ranged from cut stone to flagstone to brick and sometimes included combinations of all three. Frequently ornamented with small-scale sculpture, and almost always framed with heavy plantings that screened the view into the area beyond, Shipman's stairs usually functioned as elements of a larger picture rather than main events in the visual field.

Sketch for brick walk,
Philip B. Jennings garden,
Bennington, Vt., 1914.
RMC-Cornell Univ. Library

The Gardens of Ellen Biddle Shipman

Steps, A. Ludlow Kramer garden, Westbury, N.Y., 1920. Photo Mattie Edwards Hewitt, 1923. RMC-Cornell Univ. Library

Terrace steps, Clark Williams garden, Greenwich, Conn., 1925. Photo Harry G. Healy, 1935. RMC-Cornell Univ. Library

Walled garden with bronze figure by Anne Coleman Ladd, Holden McGinley estate, Milton, Mass. 1925. Photo Herbert W. Gleason, 1932. RMC-Cornell Univ. Library

Another modest commission, though larger than Avalon, was a job that came from Mrs. Holden McGinley of Milton, Massachusetts, in 1925. A recent divorcee, McGinley was heiress to the *Cleveland Plain Dealer* fortune; she may have met Shipman in Cleveland on one of her many jobs there.[7] The site posed an interesting problem and elicited an imaginative design solution. Massive stands of trees were grouped behind and to the west of the commanding white-washed-brick Colonial Revival house by Bigelow and Wadsworth. The property sloped gently to the south—toward open meadows and the Blue Hills. To take advantage of the view, Shipman created a two-part plan that first coaxed visitors across the lawn into the walled garden and then shifted attention ninety degrees, outward to the hills. The enclosed garden was entered through one of three gates in a brick wall; each gate opened to a different compartment. The uppermost, at the north end, was level with the house lawn; the middle garden was two steps lower; the third, at the south end, was two steps lower still. Each garden had its own character, but the three were similar enough to harmonize.

The long, narrow greensward of the middle garden was flanked by perennial borders and low walls with posts covered by climbing roses. One magazine writer recorded her impressions of the area in 1933: "Here a veritable tapestry was woven with tulips, shading from lightest to deepest pink, with the dark

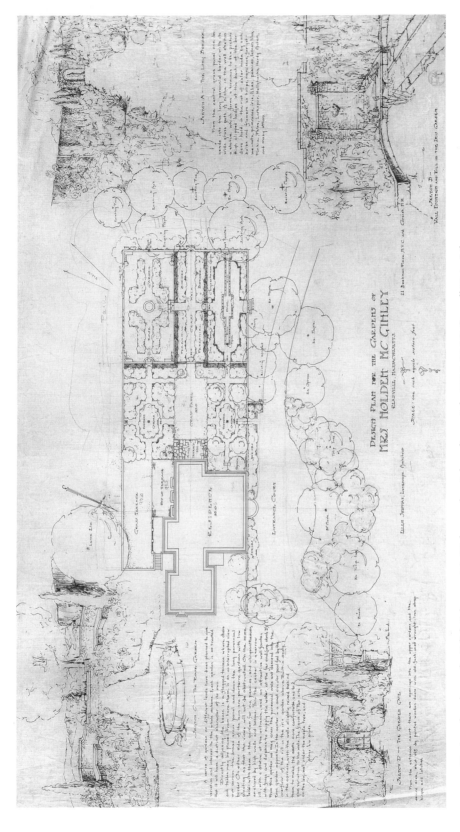

Design plan drawn by Edith Schryver, McGinley garden, ink on linen, July 1925. RMC-Cornell Univ. Library

Rill in peony, iris, and chrysanthemum garden, McGinley garden, 1925. Photo Herbert W. Gleason, 1932. RMC-Cornell Univ. Library

Edwin Lutyens and Gertrude Jekyll, Deanery Garden, Sonning-on-Thames, Berkshire, 1899. From Jekyll and Weaver, *Gardens for Small Country Houses* (London, 1912)

notes under double-flowering peach trees, pansies, *Phlox divaricata*, espaliered fruits, the pearlbush, and flowering almonds. Here was gay and shimmering color flung to the sun in profusion, but held within the bounds of visual harmony. Here were contrast of form and texture and irregularity of height, but here also was order, given by the carefully massed and interwoven colors and the continuing background of whitewashed brick wall."[8]

The upper garden was more simply planted. A bluestone-edged rill was set into the lawn; peony, chrysanthemum, and iris filled beds around the perimeter of the lawn. A variety of flowering shrubs and cedar added architectural heft to the composition. Again, Shipman found design inspiration in the work Lutyens and Jekyll, who popularized the use of rills. The one in the McGinley garden strongly resembles the watercourse in Deanery Garden, illustrated in Jekyll and Weaver's *Gardens for Small Country Houses*. Shipman's rill, however, bears only a distant spatial relationship to the main house, whereas Lutyens and Jekyll tied the two closely together.

The lower garden was given over to roses. Standard and bush roses, hybrid teas and hybrid perpetuals in shades of apricot, copper, and yellow tumbled in profusion. Golden Salmon polyanthas were clustered around the pool and lotus-leaf fountain.[9] The westward view to the hills through the unceremonious opening in the wall invited the imagination into the pastoral scene beyond, the garden outside the garden.

Pool with lotus fountain, McGinley garden, 1925. Photo Herbert W. Gleason, 1932. RMC-Cornell Univ. Library

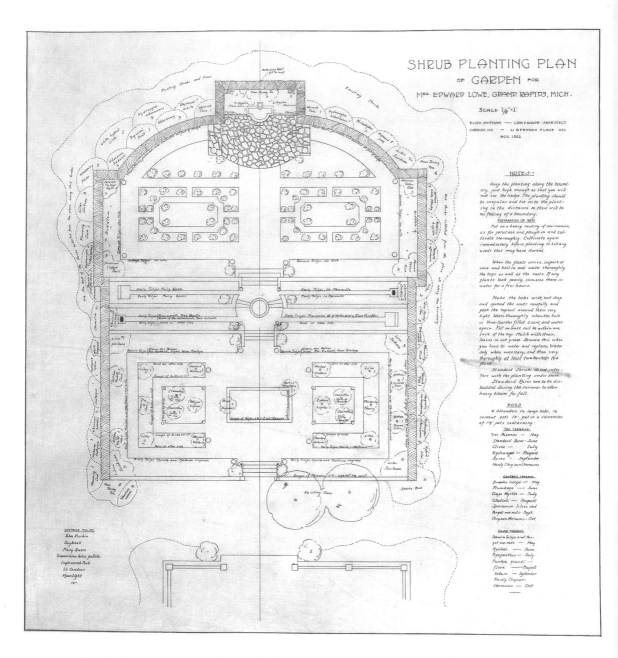

Shrub planting plan, Holmdene, Edward Lowe estate, Grand Rapids, Mich., ink on linen, August 1922. RMC-Cornell Univ. Library

Several of Shipman's projects caught the attention of the eminent garden writer Louisa Yeomans (Mrs. Francis) King, who praised her as a "creator of poetic and beautiful gardens all over this land." (Gertrude Jekyll seems to be the only other designer to have so captured King's enthusiasm.) One of the volumes in King's Little Garden series featured Shipman's design for the Pruyn sisters as a frontispiece, identifying it as an "illuminating example of what can be done with a small piece of ground." About 1923, Shipman gave an on-site, verbal consultation to King at the author's own Alma, Michigan, garden; her planting suggestions were happily adopted.[10]

In 1928, King wrote an article for *Country Life in America* about the garden Shipman designed for Edward Lowe in Grand Rapids, Michigan. Reassuring her readers that "no longer do people feel that in going to the Middle West they exile themselves from all that is worth while in the arts," King revealed her sense of the hegemony of the East coast in the garden world. One wonders whether O. C. Simonds, the prominent landscape architect who had laid out the eighty-acre estate twenty years earlier, and, like King, a Michigander, was amused. King's

Terrace and *Mercury* pool, Lowe garden, 1921. Photo Mattie Edwards Hewitt, c. 1927. RMC-Cornell Univ. Library

Rectangular pool, Lowe garden, 1921. Photo Mattie Edwards Hewitt, c. 1927. RMC-Cornell Univ. Library

interpretation of Shipman's design as English—the article was titled "An English Country Place in Michigan"—reflected the widespread opinion that any sophisticated planting in America must have been copied from England. But Shipman's innovative mix of plants and the sharp contrasts in height, texture, and shape set a more idiosyncratic tone than that of her British colleagues. The centerpiece of Shipman's three-tiered scheme was a formal pool visible from the upper house terrace. As in her design for the Brewster pool, Shipman took advantage of the architectural form as a foil for her planting. "Heucheras, sedums, statices, hostas, violas, irises, and a few stocks mark the edges," wrote King.[11] Hewitt's photographs for the article also record delphinium, and, in a most unusual combination, a cluster of woodland fern where the pool was shaded by a hawthorn. The oddly stimulating juxtapositions had the authority necessary to stand up to the surrounding plantings.

The Gardens of Ellen Biddle Shipman

August border, Lowe garden, 1921. Photo Mattie Edwards Hewitt, c. 1927. RMC-Cornell Univ.
Library

Square pool with *Pan*, Clark Williams garden, Greenwich, Conn., 1925.
Photo Harry G. Healy, 1935. RMC-Cornell Univ. Library

Brick walkways leading off the upper terrace were bordered more conventionally. "Alyssum, phloxes in wonderful array, ageratum, annual asters, zinnias, and statice," along with the foxglove, roses, and fruit standards fill Hewitt's midsummer photographs. The garden walk culminated in a shady flagstone terrace. Here a raised pool and a statue of Mercury were backed by one of the most ubiquitous native shrubs in the Midwest: box elder.

That Shipman featured pools of all descriptions in her designs was not unusual—her contemporaries were also drawn to the sound, movement, and quality of light offered by pools, ponds, rills, and fountains. But Shipman's romantic treatment of water plantings was distinctive. The complexity of the plantings and the sensuousness of their arrangements made these designs highly recognizable as hers.

Fountain terrace, Overfields, George DeForest Lord estate, Syosset, N.Y. Photo Mattie Edwards Hewitt, May 1937. RMC-Cornell Univ. Library

Oval pool, Williams garden, 1925. Photo Harry G. Healy, 1935. RMC-Cornell Univ. Library

Not all of the gardens of Shipman's rich middle period were architecturally defined. In 1926, she again went to work for the Russell Algers of Grosse Pointe, for whom she had provided planting plans years before. This time she was commissioned to do a garden for the Algers' summer home in York Harbor, Maine. Shipman abandoned the close spatial relationship between garden and house and instead nestled the garden into the rocky hillside, where it could be reached by a winding path. Here it provided an uninterrupted, more intimate view of the sea and remained out of view of the house—a world unto itself, innocent, spell-binding. The beds held a seed-packet summer garden of soft, small bloom, annuals and biennials mixed with hardy heather. The tiny flecks of color produced a shimmering, painterly composition. Dirt paths edged with stone connected the garden's lower edge with an overlook area bounded by a picket fence. In spirit,

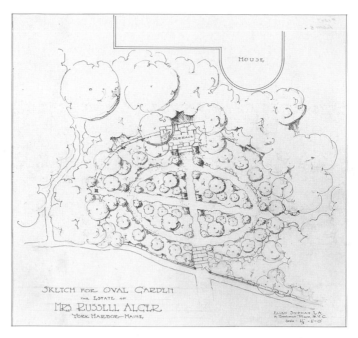

Sketch for oval garden, Russell A. Alger estate, York Harbor, Me.,
ink on tracing paper, c. 1927. RMC-Cornell Univ. Library

Old-fashioned flower garden, Alger garden, 1926. Photo MacLaughlass.
RMC-Cornell Univ. Library

Path through garden to shore, Alger garden, 1926. Photo MacLaughlass. RMC-Cornell Univ. Library

the vacation garden could not have differed more sharply from its year-round counterpart in Michigan. The design typified Shipman's departure from the world of classicism. No vestiges of the columns, fountains, and walls that defined and dominated estate designs of the period were to be found in this supple creation. Shipman's confidence was increasing. So, too, was her sense that design need not draw attention to itself to be exquisite: in fact, she was, apparently, concluding just the opposite.

CHAPTER SEVEN

THE BORDER

SHIPMAN USED borders to spectacular effect in the majority of her garden projects, varying them according to their role in the overall design, her clients' taste in plants, available staff—no garden feature was more demanding—and her own imagination. Use of the border was not, however, universal among Shipman's contemporaries, some of whom viewed them as part of an amateur tradition rather than as an artistic vehicle. Marian Coffin used them sparingly, as did Shipman's West coast colleagues Florence Yoch and Lucille Council, who, like Coffin, were more interested in inventing new features than in exploring the potential of old ones. Beatrix Farrand did incorporate the border effectively in many of her gardens, but it was not a central point of departure for her work. Fletcher Steele for the most part avoided the border in favor of bold experiments in color, texture, and plant mass (and on those occasions when he did use herbaceous borders, he asked a woman assistant to draw up the planting plans.)

American homeowners of the period, on the other hand, loved borders. No feature was more common in the backyard plan, partly because it offered a simple and effective means of growing many different flowers—and flowers, of course, were the motivation for most home gardens. Shipman's genuine enthusiasm for horticulture and her respect for clients' involvement in their own gardens attracted business and put her in contact with people whose interests she shared and whose lives her design talent could enrich. "I never am quite satisfied until there is some place that I can walk between flowers," she wrote one client.[1]

Within the narrow confines of the genre, Shipman discovered extraordinary variety. She used the flower border to focus and narrate the experience of a garden, almost like a soliloquy in a play. Even a brief survey of Shipman's borders

Beatrix Farrand, herbaceous borders, Dumbarton Oaks, Washington, D.C., early 1930s.
Courtesy The Trustees of Harvard University, Dumbarton Oaks

Fletcher Steele, borders, Standish Backus estate, Grosse Pointe Shores, Mich., c. 1930.
Fletcher Steele Manuscript Collection, SUNYCESF, Syracuse, N.Y.

Borders, Picket Farm, A. Ludlow Kramer estate, Westbury, N.Y., 1920. Photo Mattie Edwards Hewitt, 1923. RMC-Cornell Univ. Library

Double borders, Angus Smith garden, Detroit, Mich. Photo Shipman office, 1929. RMC-Cornell Univ. Library

reveals a wide range of investigation. The textures of the Kramer garden, for example, were strong and coarse, the ephemeral plantings for Angus Smith, simple and sweet. The narrow grass path in the Murray Sales garden, where borders were featured as the garden's main theme, was intimate and informal; a walk down it, ankle-deep in flowers, brought visitors to a ginger step around an elm tree that grew—certainly was planted—right in the middle of it. Some designs were more interesting for the contradictions they embraced. A long formal border against the south brick wall of the McGinley terrace was accompanied by a dirt path, edged in broken stone, perhaps a quotation from Gertrude Jekyll's spring border at Munstead Wood. Like Jekyll's, Shipman's design skills developed from practical experience: her ability to shape a garden picture in her mind evolved from years of actually digging, lifting, separating, and sinking plants in the dirt.

Shipman's intuitive understanding of the emotional importance of lush borders to her women clients—including Clara Ford, Gertrude Seiberling, and Elizabeth Mather—would prove crucial to her success. These women, and many others, sought opportunities for intimate interaction with their gardens and looked to the domestically based activities of planning, planting, cultivating, cutting, and arranging flowers for meaningful bonds that extended beyond aesthetic appreciation. In the case of Ford, Seiberling, and Mather, large residential

View of garden, Murray Sales estate, Grosse Pointe, Mich. Photo George W. Hance, c. 1926. RMC-Cornell Univ. Library

The Gardens of Ellen Biddle Shipman

Double borders, Sales garden. Photo George W. Hance, c. 1926. RMC-Cornell Univ. Library

Spring border, Holden McGinley garden, Milton, Mass., 1925. Photo Herbert W. Gleason, 1932. RMC-Cornell Univ. Library

landscapes had been designed by prominent landscape architects whose skills— and interests—fell short of border design. After years of dissatisfaction with perfunctory plantings, they summoned Ellen Shipman to create more vibrant plantings within an existing framework.

Twelve years before Shipman went to work for Henry and Clara Ford in 1927, they had hired Chicago-based landscape architect Jens Jensen to plan a two-thousand-acre estate in Dearborn, Michigan. Jensen's monumental and poetic design featured long, sinuous meadows and craggy rockwork bordering the Rouge River. Formality found a place, too. The Great Meadow was to be viewed from a balustraded terrace on one end of the long house; a small terrace garden adjoining the other end was the site of a formal rose garden. Henry loved the landscape, but Clara Ford found the scarcity of flowers frustrating. Although Jensen's meadows offered fleeting pleasures of the most refined sort, they did not provide the big, bold flower borders or the intimate horticultural contact that

Clara wanted. In 1925, she hired Herbert J. Kellaway and rose specialist Harriett Foote to lay out an immense rose garden—smack dab in the center of one of Jensen's meadows. Jensen exploded when he saw the results and demanded that the ASLA reprimand Kellaway for interfering with the integrity of his work. When they refused, Jensen resigned his membership. Henry and Jens eventually reconciled, but Jens and Clara never found the warmth of their earlier relations.

Shipman was invited to Fair Lane two years after the Kellaway blowup to design perennial plantings for Jensen's original rose garden—now that Clara Ford no longer needed it. She suggested reconfiguring the beds in the small rectangular space and adding new plantings (including herbaceous perennials, shrubs, and small trees), a teahouse, grand iron gates, and a small pool.

Shipman's planting notes for "Mrs. Ford's Garden" shed light on her sense of the garden as an entity that exists in time, the slow-motion unfolding of an art. The predominant colors of the lavish display were blues, whites, and occasional glints of yellow, a color scheme that Shipman used extensively. She

Clara Ford in flower garden at Fair Lane, Dearborn, Mich., May 1939. From the Collections of Henry Ford Museum and Greenfield Village, Dearborn

Elizabeth Ring Mather at Gwinn, Cleveland, Ohio, late 1930s. Courtesy William Gwinn Mather Papers, Gwinn Archives

The Border   115

explained her planting design technique in a letter to Clara Ford: "I usually use one main plant at a time to dominate in the garden, beginning with the bulbs, and the other plants that are used at that time are complimentary [sic] to the dominant one." April and May were given over to bulbs as well as other spring flowers for contrast. "The next main plant which dominates the garden," Shipman wrote, "would be the iris, beginning with the earlier varieties and running into the German iris." "From the iris," Shipman wrote under the heading "late June," "we would run into the early and later peonies." In July: "Before the peonies have gone, the early larkspur comes, and then the larkspur completely dominates the garden." And August: "Before the larkspur is gone, the early Phlox comes." And September: "By the time the phlox is gone, the autumn garden has come and the later phlox, set off by the autumn flowers, the hardy asters (hybrid), Boltonia, the Eupatoriums, agerotoides and coledestinum, the later aconitum, anemone hupehensis, dahlias, which have been set in to take the place of the Delphiniums, that were cut back, Gladiolus, Hibiscus, Plumbago, Sedums." October: "By late autumn, the anemone japonica and the late hardy asters and chrysanthemums, and the very late aconitum and Pyrethrum. If the Nepeta and Lavendula have been cut back after the spring bloom, they will bloom again in the late autumn." Happy relations between Mrs. Shipman and Mrs. Ford extended into the 1930s, as the landscape architect returned several times to advise on planting in the area.[2]

Shipman's involvement at Stan Hywet Hall in Akron, Ohio, during 1928, reflected a similar wish on the part of a woman client to grow beautiful flowers in formal garden settings. In this case, however, it was the estate's original designer, Warren Manning, who suggested the revision of his own planting. Manning's 1911 design for Frank and Gertrude Seiberling's three-thousand-acre estate was primarily naturalistic in style and inspiration, organized around a dramatic quarry that offered unusual planting opportunities and a varied and picturesque wilderness. The design also included several agrarian features, an English landskip–inspired front lawn, and several formal elements, most of which were worked out in consultation with the architect, Charles Schneider: birch and London plane tree allées, terraces, perennial borders, and the walled English Garden. A Japanese garden, designed by T. R. Otsuka, nestled between the big quarry garden and the landscape's more formal elements. Founder of the Goodyear Tire Company, Frank Seiberling, like many successful American industrialists, was eager to spend lavish amounts of his newly acquired fortune in creating a country estate.

Of all the parts of the landscape, only the English Garden offered complete privacy. According to family memory, it was Gertrude Seiberling's favorite refuge from the tensions of running her busy household. She came to the walled garden

The Gardens of Ellen Biddle Shipman

Gertrude Seiberling in the English Garden, Stan Hywet Hall, F. A. Seiberling estate, Akron, Ohio, c. 1920. Stan Hywet Hall Archives

to escape—to think, to compose, and to talk privately with her children. Manning wrote to Frank Seiberling about the development of the estate's other features, but the discussion of the English Garden took place with Gertrude, whose word apparently was final. It was her suggestion to paint the trellises "verdigris green" and to site the walled garden so that it would be a secret, screened by shrubbery and discovered after walking through the Japanese garden.[3]

According to Manning's records, there was no planting plan to organize the roster of annuals, biennials, perennials, and vines that sounded an odd but vibrant chorus of oranges and maroons. Gertrude, a sophisticated amateur painter, tired of the combination and by 1928 decided to do something about it, suggesting specifically a "blue, yellow, pink and white garden." Manning recommended that she call in Shipman for the revision, assuring his client that he considered "her one of the best, if not the very best, Flower Garden Maker in America."[4] The accolade may well have been repeated to other of Manning's clients, including Elizabeth and William Mather, who hired Shipman a few years later for work at Gwinn.

Irene Seiberling Harrison, the youngest of the family's seven children, remembered one of Shipman's visits to Stan Hywet in 1928. Ellen and Gertrude breakfasted together as they discussed the new garden and then retired to Mrs. Seiberling's bedroom to converse uninterrupted. Irene, who was then thirty-eight years old, remembered Mrs. Shipman as "a knowledgeable person, super-educated person.... She was also very nice. Friendly, in a sense."[5] She also remembered Ellen Shipman's intensity about the task at hand.

Shipman drew up two planting plans in May 1929 which show the retention of Manning's Arts and Crafts garden architecture, including the walls, niches, paths, pools, and a fountain by the sculptor Willard Paddock. She added small ornamental trees and standards to embolden the flower beds, which were designed in the pinks, blues, and yellows Gertrude had requested. Shipman's intensive planting for these borders has been likened to a "glittering mosaic of color." Over eighty different kinds of plants were added. As in Clara Ford's garden, Shipman interwove bulbs, annuals, and perennials with heftier standards, shrubs, and trees "to cast shadows across the blooms in summer time."[6]

Nancy Seiberling in the English Garden, Stan Hywet Hall, c. 1942. Stan Hywet Hall Archives

The Gardens of Ellen Biddle Shipman

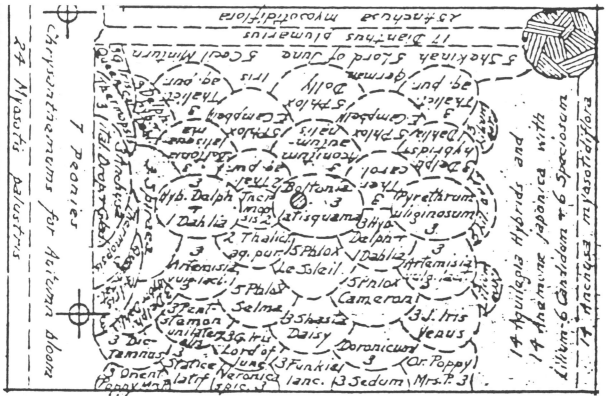

Perennial planting plan (detail) , Stan Hywet Hall, ink on linen, 11 May 1929. Stan Hywet Hall Archives

The circumstances of Shipman's work at Gwinn were only slightly different. She returned to the Cleveland estate in 1935 to design planting plans for the same beds she had made recommendations for two decades earlier. The Depression had forced cutbacks in general development and maintenance throughout the estate shortly after William Mather's 1929 marriage to Elizabeth Ireland. But by the mid-1930s, when the Mathers' finances had stabilized and the couple had decided to pursue a modest renovation of the estate grounds, Elizabeth Mather was eager to find ways to make the twenty-one-acre estate her own. It was not surprising that, as a master gardener and president of the Garden Club of Greater Cleveland, she turned her interest to the formal garden. Manning's dappled wild garden across the street offered opportunities for Thorvaldian solitude, but more of Elizabeth Mather's time and emotional energy would find an outlet in the brilliant flowering of the beds.

Shipman's recommendations for the new scheme respected the layout of Charles Platt's 1907 design but brought new complexity and spatial interest to the geometry of the walled area. As at Fair Lane, Shipman featured one type of flower to dominate each season. She retained Platt's basic color scheme of blue,

Formal garden, Gwinn, William G. Mather estate, Cleveland, Ohio, c. 1950. Photo Walter P. Bruning. Courtesy William Gwinn Mather Papers, Gwinn Archives

white, and yellow but softened it with shades of pink and peach. Her suggestion of Japanese cherries, flowering almonds, and Japanese lilacs to surround the pool was met with some concern by the Mathers, who were accustomed to the garden's openness. But before long, the sunny geometry of Platt's layout had acquired lingering shadows and mystery; Shipman had made the walled enclosure more poetic by putting three-dimensional forms into it.

Had Shipman's client correspondence survived, her specific relationships with her women clients and her role in creating settings in response to their imaginative selves would no doubt be clearer. Nonetheless, there is no question that Shipman's services invariably led to garden spaces that offered far more to their owners than settings for tea. At a time when women's expressiveness was not encouraged—at home or in the world generally—flower gardens provided female clients with sensuous havens and a grounding link to seasonal rhythms and cycles. Shipman's power to facilitate the development of such gardens suggests that she may have played a highly charged emotional as well as aesthetic role in the lives of her women clients.

The Gardens of Ellen Biddle Shipman

View into pergola, Gwinn, c. 1950. Photo Walter P. Bruning. Courtesy William Gwinn Mather Papers, Gwinn Archives

Vista to pool, Penwood, Carll Tucker estate, Mount Kisco, N.Y., 1926. Photo Harry G. Healy, late 1930s. RMC-Cornell Univ. Library

CHAPTER EIGHT

A GRANDER SCOPE

SEVERAL COMMISSIONS from the mid- to late-1920s involved more extensive architectural structures than any previous and thus catapulted Shipman into a new level of design involvement. American gardens were becoming increasingly exotic as the affluent traveled abroad and returned with grand cultural pretensions. Shipman responded by incorporating a variety of architectural styles, including Colonial Revival, Italian, Mediterranean, and British, into her work. The aesthetic success of these more architecturally determined gardens rested on Shipman's hard-won ability to integrate large spaces and handsome detailing with her own planting style. Interestingly, because Shipman's expressive style had evolved outside of the prevailing influences, it may well have been the more original for not having been shaped by the European tastes that dominated so many of her colleagues' development.

The most recognizably "Shipmanesque" of these commissions was Penwood, the Carll Tucker estate in Mount Kisco, New York, not far from Wampus, the much-photographed Magee garden. Shipman worked with the Tuckers from 1926 on, returning at regular intervals to adjust and augment the design. The garden began at a distance from the house and was bounded on the southwest edge by a rustic Italian pergola or, more properly, loggia, since one side of the structure was walled. Thick stucco pillars supported a cedar trellis, evoking images of the sunny Tuscan campagna. These images were, of course, gleaned from books—Shipman had not yet traveled to Italy. Huge slabs of fieldstone paved the pergola floor and major paths through the big flower garden, resulting in an arresting contrast as the chunky architectural forms exaggerated the delicacy of the plantings.

Parterre garden and pergola, Tucker garden, 1926. Photo Mattie Edwards Hewitt, 1927.
RMC-Cornell Univ. Library

Pool, Tucker garden, 1926. Photo Mattie Edwards Hewitt, 1927. RMC-Cornell Univ. Library

A parterre garden stretched in front of the pergola, adjoined by a square flower garden. A pool marked the center of the square, its raised coping an ingenious, urgent afterthought—because of a mismeasurement, the pool had been plumbed about six inches too high. Shipman's assistant, Eleanor Christie, remembered the panic over the additional expense a revision would have entailed, observing: "Of course you don't just dig out a pool and redo it." She and Louise Payson solved the problem by using three levels of coping instead of the single layer originally planned; Shipman, according to Christie, "was thrilled to death" with the result.[1] So, too, apparently, were the legions of magazine photographers who found the little pool irresistible. The design was copied in several other gardens of the period, including Shipman's own at Brook Place.

After spring tulips and narcissus faded, a heftier crop of foxgloves, delphinium, peonies, columbine, and astilbe filled the garden's beds. The flower masses reached about four to five feet, effectively swallowing spring standards of wiste-

September border, Tucker garden, 1926. Photo Harry G. Healy, late 1930s. RMC-Cornell Univ. Library

A Grander Scope   125

ria and lilacs. In September, monkshood, Japanese anemones, dahlias, hardy asters, and gladiolus succeeded the taller subjects, and the standards once again emerged from the masses, the altheas now in bloom. *House Beautiful* praised the Tucker garden for its "luxuriant growth which makes each division a self-contained unit with its own interest, but composing with the others by means of pleasant vistas."[2]

Shipman mixed lacy spring bloom with tall evergreen spires to make the transition to the greenery beyond. In one plan a sequestered wild garden and pond are indicated to the west. A more diminutive scale was explored in the tiny violets, violas, dianthus, and dwarf iris tucked amid the stones of the pool coping. Shipman returned to Penwood after a hiatus caused by World War II to revise the garden and suggested a reduced maintenance plan. Over 150 drawings and documents were generated, an indication of the seriousness with which the clients regarded their landscape.

In 1924, Shipman again stretched beyond her idiomatic approach when she was hired by Evander B. Schley in Far Hills, New Jersey, to create a series of gardens "in the Spanish mood."[3] The house by Peabody, Wilson and Brown, also of Spanish inspiration and pre-dating her work there, was perhaps the lone example

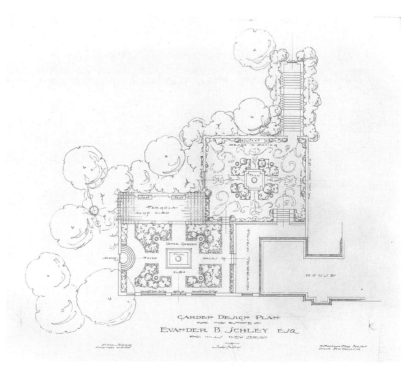

Garden design plan, Evander B. Schley estate, Far Hills, N.J., ink on tissue, c. 1924. RMC-Cornell Univ. Library

The Gardens of Ellen Biddle Shipman

Paved terrace, Schley garden, 1924. Photo John Wallace Gilles, c. 1930. RMC-Cornell Univ.
Library

Tiled pool in lower garden, Schley garden, 1924. Photo John Wallace Gilles, c. 1930. RMC-Cornell Univ. Library

of the architectural type among Shipman's client residences. The red-tiled roof and heavy stucco walls that defined Spanish revival architecture were not common in the Northeast and Midwest, where Shipman did most of her work.

Shipman's predeliction for strongly axial, walled gardens did not need much adjustment for this job, since it coincided with the traditional Spanish approach to garden making. But the commission also offered new opportunities for experiments with exotic embellishment, and these Shipman approached with unusual relish. Elaborate paving patterns (in New England–style brick), ceramic tilework, terra-cotta pots, espaliered roses, and near-tropical plants (including *Agapanthus*, evidently overwintered indoors) summoned the unrestrained sensuality of a Spanish courtyard garden. Shipman's job notes indicate the use of large cedars and flowering trees to "simulate the cypress and fruit trees of Spain and give grateful shade." A less voluptuous upper garden organized around a central pool with four splashing jets featured enormous *tinjajones* (Spanish oil jars) at the corners of the beds.

The Gardens of Ellen Biddle Shipman

East elevation, Chatham Manor, Daniel B. Devore estate, Fredericksburg,
Va., 1924. Photo Frances Benjamin Johnston, c. 1927. Library of Congress

The same year, 1924, Shipman was in Fredericksburg, Virginia, to work up
an elaborate Colonial Revival garden for Chatham, a 1721 house undergoing
restoration by architect Oliver H. Clarke. The historical importance of the
house—George Washington spent much of his early life at Chatham and Robert
E. Lee met and married Mary Custis there—would have interested Shipman.
The charge from her clients, Colonel and Mrs. Daniel B. Devore, was to create a
period garden. Shipman was apparently pleased with the result, for she later
wrote, "Most people thought the garden had been there when the house was
restored." In truth, the site had been a cornfield.[4]

Shipman was so thoroughly steeped in the forms and feeling of the Colonial
Revival garden, then at the peak of its popularity, that she scarcely needed to
reflect consciously on them—in this sense Chatham was simply a grander version of her usual, more modestly scaled work. In this rich design, she managed to
create a believable Colonial spirit and a luxuriousness not typical of such gardens. Avoiding the tight precision that so often characterized period imitation,
Shipman emulated something much more elusive: the relaxed, unreflective irregularity that develops in gardens over time.

One writer recorded her impressions in 1926: "On the right of the pathway,
nearest the terrace, was that part of the garden which, starting in a formal way
with arches and box edgings, had then abandoned the well-laid plan of the gar-

Vista with sculpture, Devore garden, 1924. Photo Frances Benjamin Johnston, c. 1927. Library of Congress

dener and run riot, making the garden its own. And so inspirational was its plan—with its mass of apricot, rose, and white *Phlox drummondi* spreading a lovely carpet over the garden beds and reaching beyond, its miniature fruit-trees and tendriled arches growing in willful pleasure—that the fair gardener, putting beauty before order, allowed it to remain and acknowledged her defeat."[5] Despite the writer's enthusiasm for the relaxed charm of Chatham, she failed to mention Ellen Shipman's role in its design. Years later, however, in 1938, the garden was featured on the cover of the annual garden week guidebook of the Garden Club of Virginia. Shipman's design lasted only until World War II, when

The Gardens of Ellen Biddle Shipman

the landscape architect Ralph Griswold simplified it by removing the labor-intensive perennial beds and adding more boxwood.[6] Like most of her contemporaries, Shipman ultimately watched the majority of her landscape designs disappear, victims of changing taste and shifting fortunes.

Somewhat more focused than these historical amalgamations was Shipman's involvement with the Arts and Crafts movement. Centered in the Cotswolds, the approach was developed by a group of architects and designers who worked in a

Perennial border and pergola, Devore garden, 1924. Photo Frances Benjamin Johnston, c. 1927. Library of Congress

A Grander Scope   131

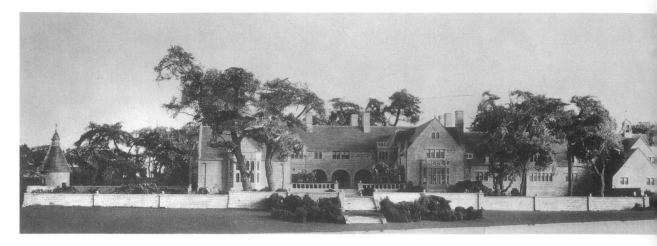

Model of Salvage estate, 1926. Photo Mattie Edwards Hewitt, c. 1926. RMC-Cornell Univ. Library

vernacular architectural style as opposed to the Tudor-derived style promoted by the formalists. The pages of *Country Life* magazine and numerous British books of the period show many examples that exhibited the two fundamental aspects of the Arts and Crafts garden: the collaboration of architect and craftsman working in regional building traditions and the close alliance of house, garden, and decorative arts.[7] In America, the Arts and Crafts garden took on regional shadings, with a strong emphasis on handcrafted decorative arts and use of local building materials and garden architecture.[8] Many eastern and midwestern estates of the period, whose surroundings resembled the gently rolling Cotswold hills, reflected this influence. Chestnut Hill, Pennsylvania, and other areas rich in local stone were particularly well suited to it, but the Cotswold style was also transplanted to unlikely settings, such as Long Island's Gold Coast, where it expressed a taste for exoticism rather than for regionalism. Shipman created two particularly significant Arts and Crafts–inspired gardens there during the decade.

The first was for Rynwood, the manor house estate commissioned from Roger H. Bullard by Samuel A. Salvage in 1926. It was one of Shipman's largest and most important jobs to date. The site plan, likely conceived in consultation with the architect, included a large courtyard, a service courtyard, a terrace, three separate formal gardens, a swimming pool, a tennis court, and several acres of surrounding fields. A photograph of a detailed model (the only example in Shipman's archives) shows the architectural components and plantings of the estate.

The garden's major architectural ornaments were a round, slate-roofed dovecote, designed by Shipman in response to Bullard's Tudor-inspired architectural detailing, and a teahouse modeled after a small building at Snowshill Manor in the Cotswolds.[9] She placed the dovecote opposite the teahouse, midway down

The Gardens of Ellen Biddle Shipman

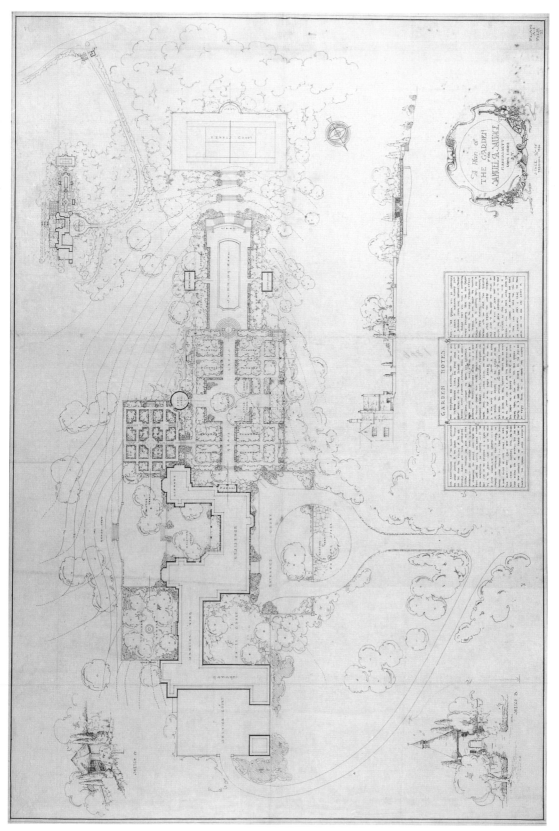

General design plan for Rynwood, Samuel A. Salvage estate, Glen Head, N.Y., ink on linen, February 1926. RMC-Cornell Univ. Library

Dovecote, Salvage garden, 1926. Photo Harry G. Healy, 1935. RMC-Cornell Univ. Library

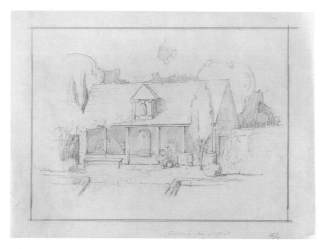

Sketch for teahouse, Salvage garden, pencil on trace, 1926.
RMC-Cornell Univ. Library

Teahouse walk, Salvage garden, 1926. Photo Mattie Edwards Hewitt,
May 1934. RMC-Cornell Univ. Library

Pool, Salvage garden, 1926. Photo Harry G. Healy, 1935. RMC-Cornell Univ. Library

Flagstone path, Salvage garden, 1926. Photo Harry G. Healy, 1935. RMC-Cornell Univ. Library

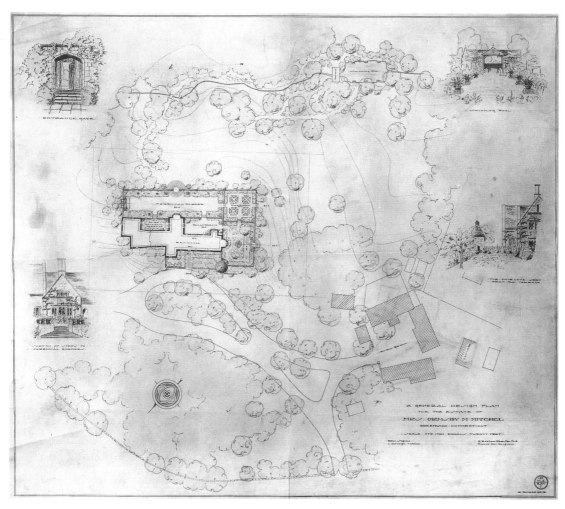

General design plan drawn by Irma Berger, Ormsby M. Mitchell estate, Greenwich, Conn., pen and colored pencil on trace, 12 November 1929. RMC-Cornell Univ. Library

the west side of a large walled garden, where it would also serve as an anchor for a smaller garden, thereby capitalizing twice on its distinctive silhouette and old English charm. The center of the teahouse garden was marked by a circular, *Bergenia*-edged pool and shaded by an old apple tree. Fruit-tree allées, boxwood-edged beds filled with masses of mixed perennials, and enormous hydrangeas followed examples from simple Cornish gardens and also contributed to the spatial definition of the area. The quirky eclecticism of Shipman's planting design—in this case drawn from Italian, French, and English gardens—was perhaps its single most defining "American" quality.

Shipman's garden for the Ormsby Mitchells in Greenwich, Connecticut, begun three years after the Salvage estate, also expressed Arts and Crafts ideals and attracted the praise of American critics—"no Cotswold house that we know has had the advantage of such delightful gardening," wrote one of them

Millstone terrace, Mitchell garden, 1929. Photo Harry G. Healy, c. 1937. RMC-Cornell Univ. Library

Rose garden and terrace, Mitchell garden, 1929. Photo Harry G. Healy, c. 1937. RMC-Cornell Univ. Library

proudly."[10] The design marked a new level of assurance in her work. Here Shipman combined a spatial plan of unprecedented cohesiveness with unusually spare plantings, most of which related strongly to the garden architecture and also recalled English prototypes—ivy-covered garden walls, for example. Yet some planting passages achieved an unexpected and original character.

A November 1929 drawing by Shipman's assistant Irma Berger shows the overall design scheme. A lawn terrace at the back of the house was flanked by perennial borders; a walled, paved terrace at the south end of the house, and sited directly on axis with it, had a small octagonal pool in the center and a dovecote-toolhouse (similar to the Salvages', which she had designed three years earlier) placed at the intersection of this area and a formal, walled entry court. Filling the corner between the paved terrace and lawn terrace was a square rose garden, marked by two intersecting grass walks. The architect, Alfred Hopkins, used stone from the Greenwich vicinity in the Cotswold-style house and all the outbuildings. One of these was a small house that held a studio and open hearth fireplace. Shipman's unusually restrained plantings tied these separate structures, terraces, and paved courts together.

Dining room terrace and playroom, Mitchell garden, 1929. Photo Harry G. Healy, c. 1937. RMC-Cornell Univ. Library

Dovecote, Mitchell garden, 1929. Photo Harry G. Healy, c. 1937. RMC-Cornell Univ. Library

The sculptural proportions of the garden areas reflected the masses of the house and sounded a new note of authority in Shipman's body of work. The spatial clarity of these areas was unusually bold, a result, in part, of the strong walls and clear changes of level. Shipman's preoccupation with paths as spatial determinants was nowhere in evidence. She had adopted a thoroughly three-dimensional approach to space making. The low-rising circular steps leading from the dovecote terrace to the lawn, modeled after traditional English garden steps, were also sculptural. The repetition of the curve in the steps, dovecote, openwork walls, and octagonal pool established a rhythm that pulled the parts into a whole.

Because each area in the Mitchell scheme had its own definitive character, transitions from one to another were distinct. Most memorable in the several vignettes captured in Harry Healy's photographs is the pairing of an old wisteria and a small pool that it shaded—and dwarfed—beneath. The unexpected match saved the scene from the generic formulas that made so many landscapes of the period more perfunctory than inspired.

Wisteria pool, Mitchell garden, 1929. Photo Harry G. Healy, c. 1937. RMC-Cornell Univ. Library

CHAPTER NINE

WILD GARDENS

IN THE SEVERAL naturalistic gardens Shipman designed through the 1920s and 1930s, she may have been influenced by Warren Manning, with whom she shared a close, collegial relationship. Manning frequently coaxed his clients to set aside portions of their properties as woodland, for hiking, horseback riding, and even boating. Shipman would have seen Manning's quarry garden at Stan Hywet in the late 1920s, when she was there working on the English Garden, and the large wild garden that he laid out at Gwinn beginning in 1914. Many other landscape architects promoted wild gardens as well. Certain of them, such as Jens Jensen, advocated for broad, primarily naturalistic landscape treatments of entire estates, but almost every American landscape architect involved with residential commissions found occasion to create areas of designed wilderness.

A comparison between Shipman's wild garden efforts and those of two of her colleagues illuminates a key factor in her garden making generally. Percival Gallagher of Olmsted Brothers was typical of many designers, including Shipman, who introduced carefully crafted wilderness into Beaux Arts–influenced designs. The heavily planted ravine garden by Gallagher at Oldfields, the Indianapolis estate of Hugh and Jessie Landon, was, like Shipman's gardens, essentially ornamental in inspiration. The rocky hillside setting represented an opportunity to introduce lavish plantings that—to Gallagher's eye anyway—appeared spontaneous regardless of their exotic pedigree. It is likely that this type of wild garden was inspired by William Robinson's book *The Wild Garden,* which enjoyed a wide readership in the United States.

Warren Manning, Wild Garden, Stan Hywet Hall, early 1920s. Stan Hywet Hall Archives

Percival Gallagher, ravine garden, Oldfields, J. K. Lilly Jr. estate, Indianapolis, after 1932. Indianapolis Museum of Art

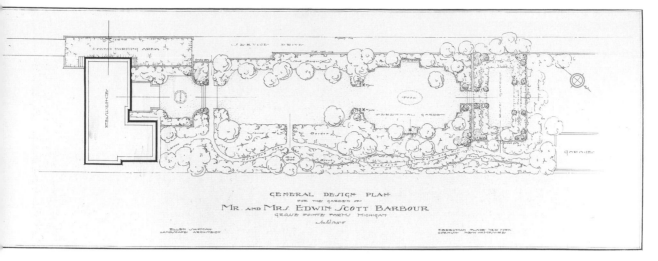

General design plan, Edwin Scott Barbour garden, Grosse Pointe Farms, Mich., ink on trace, 1927. RMC-Cornell Univ. Library

Manning's approach, by contrast, derived from the idea that the wild garden was embedded in nature and could, through careful pruning, be extracted from it. Although Manning also recommended extensive new plantings and did not distinguish—as did his midwestern colleague Jensen—between native and non-native species, he emphasized respect for the existing features of the site, and would have been loath to construct false features such as waterfalls and pools. While Shipman's approach more closely resembled that of the Olmsted firm, she may nevertheless have been inspired by Manning's example and his belief that the aesthetic experience of the wild garden was one his clients would enjoy. And although Shipman's wild gardens do not figure among her best work, they reflect the essence of her garden making: the idea of the garden as an artistic creation, an artifice.

In addition to offering an aesthetic alternative to formality, many of Shipman's wild gardens also filled pivotal design roles. On a small suburban lot owned by the Edwin Scott Barbours in Grosse Pointe Farms, she developed a long shrub and birch garden as a screen to a neighboring property. Using the fieldstone path and accompanying rill and bird-bath pools as a spine, Shipman organized the plantings on either side to create a narrow stroll garden. The small-scale plantings among the irregular rockwork included alpines, bulbs, and ground-hugging thyme in seemingly haphazard, "natural" arrangement, but to knowing eyes, the lush floral display undoubtedly struck a more deliberately crafted note.

In her 1926 design for Mrs. Henry V. Greenough, in Brookline, Massachusetts, Shipman combined formal and wild gardens in a compressed urban setting. Mrs. Greenough, Mrs. Windsor White's sister-in-law, may have met Shipman through her or one of Shipman's other Cleveland clients. The formal area

Naturalistic pool and walk, Barbour garden, 1927. Photo
Thomas Ellison, June 1936. RMC-Cornell Univ. Library

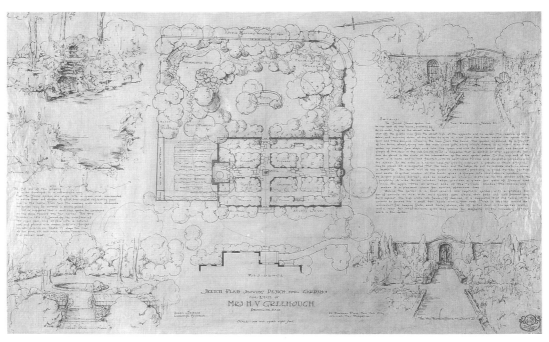

Sketch plan drawn by Edith Schryver, H. V. Greenough garden, Brookline, Mass., ink on linen,
January 1926. RMC-Cornell Univ. Library

Naturalistic pool with native plants, Greenough garden, 1926. Photo Dorothy Jarvis Studio, c. 1931. RMC-Cornell Univ. Library

was given Shipman's prototypal layout: a rectangular space divided by walks with axial accents at either end, a garden house and sculpture. Horticultural interest and color were planned for all seasons—masses of bulbs in spring, heliotrope and petunias in summer, asters and boltonia in the autumn, juniper and pachysandra through winter. Beyond the formal area lay an informal lawn surrounded by trees and shrubs, and beyond this, a woodland with a pool and miniature waterfall. High brick walls surrounded the densely canopied garden. Again, Shipman's idealized plant scheme was more exotic than anything that would have occurred naturally. The palette included a wide variety of native and non-native species, as one writer noted: "Mountain-ash, arborvitae, hemlock, dogwood, laurel rhododendron and viburnum ... big leaf saxifrage, calla lilies, waterlilies, iris, eupatorium, Shortia, and other native creeping wood-and water-loving plants."[1] That Shipman *intended* these gardens to seem natural is beyond question; but she was also aware of the complexities of the design task at hand. "You are trying to copy nature," she wrote, "her pocket has no bottom, and her lavishness is unbound, ... her art of arrangement is the art of the Lord."[2]

Wild Gardens   147

Wild garden and stone terrace, Willard M. Clapp estate, Cleveland, Ohio, 1926. Photo Thomas Ellison. RMC-Cornell Univ. Library

The wild garden that Shipman designed for the Willard Clapp estate in a suburban setting in Cleveland Heights, Ohio, was also typical of her work in the genre. (One of Shipman's 1927 construction drawings referred to a plan "supplied by Manning's offices," suggesting that he provided engineering and site-planning services for the job.) Its formal counterpart, developed on axis with the large house, was typical as well; it featured a central reflecting pool and airy flower borders that recalled designs from many of Shipman's other projects. At the rear of the lawn was a naturalistic pond where irregular stones surrounding the water's edge were interplanted with a mixture of native and exotic plants, including iris, coral bells, *Bergenia,* and several varieties of thyme. Rhododendron and small specimen trees created a screen planting for the little woodland.

A more elaborate wild garden was developed for Mrs. Jonathan Bulkley in Ridgefield, Connecticut, in the late 1920s or early 1930s. Mrs. Bulkley was a prominent member and, between 1932 and 1935, president of the Garden Club of America. In Shipman's design a dense woodland backdrop was the setting for Edward McCartan's statue of Diana and a large swimming pool. Elsewhere on

The Gardens of Ellen Biddle Shipman

the property, a rocky waterfall composed a more deliberate "wilderness" and set up a dramatic mountain view. Masterfully engineered, the complex stonework waterfall and path were nonetheless mannered, theatrical beyond anything wind and water might have worn in the side of a mountain. The studied planting design—of ferns, dianthus, ajuga, campanula, iris, and other ornamentals— heightened the impossibly arcadian look of the hillside.[3]

Reflecting pool with *Diana* by Edward McCartan, Rippowam, Jonathan Bulkley estate, Ridgefield, Conn., late 1920s. Photo Mattie Edwards Hewitt, 1931. RMC-Cornell Univ. Library

Stream garden, Bulkley garden, late 1920s. Photo Mattie Edwards Hewitt, 1931. RMC-Cornell Univ. Library

In 1927 Shipman designed a wild garden design for James Parmelee, for whom she had worked fifteen years earlier with Charles Platt. Photographs of the woodland design suggest a different tone from most of her others, although planting plans record a complex scheme that, as in other designs, mixed drifts of ornamental exotics with indigenous varieties. Period images show a woodland overstory shadowing large clumps of rhododendron and opening to sun-drenched clearings. A rare sense of ease emanates from these garden pictures.

Waterfall in stream garden, Bulkley garden, late 1920s. Photo Mattie Edwards Hewitt, 1931. RMC-Cornell Univ. Library

Shipman developed one of her most extensive wild gardens during the 1930s and 1940s for Edith Stern, a New Orleans client whose enthusiasm for native plants led her to underwrite the 1934 publication of Caroline Dormon's *Wildflowers of Louisiana*. Three paths gave the garden its structure; one was designated for camellias, the other two for Louisiana iris and wildflowers. Stern consulted primarily with Dormon about the plantings, but relied on Shipman for overall design structure. John Mackenroth, Longue Vue's head gardener from 1927 to 1942, dug thousands of native plants from the woods. The iris were made to feel at home in wire-reinforced concrete beds that were periodically flooded to produce swamp conditions.[4]

Shipman designed wild gardens as discrete areas within larger residential landscapes, but she also routinely attempted to tie the formal garden to the surrounding landscape through the use of native plants and boundary wilderness. In a sense these transitional landscapes, whether copses, meadows, or shrubberies, were all wild gardens of a sort. As she later explained, "Each part [of the landscape] should lure you on and should become less and less formal until you reach the wild walk leading to the wild garden."[5]

Woodland garden, James Parmelee estate, Washington, D.C. Photo Shipman office, 1920s. RMC-Cornell Univ. Library

The Gardens of Ellen Biddle Shipman

CHAPTER TEN

THE GREAT DEPRESSION AND THE LURE OF EUROPE

AFTER LOUIS SHIPMAN departed for France in 1925, he never returned to Brook Place or to the United States. For reasons unknown, Ellen Shipman kept his study and memorabilia intact behind the secret door in the library in their Cornish home. They divorced in 1927. The following year, Louis married an actress named Lucille Watson. He died five years later, leaving a small legacy to Evan but nothing to his daughters.[1]

The stock market crash two years after her divorce had an immediate impact on Ellen Shipman's practice. During the Depression years she earned most of her living from a few extremely wealthy clients whose large fortunes weathered the economic crisis. In response to the shrinking number of residential jobs, she began to seek institutional and interior design commissions. As had Charles Platt, Shipman used her design skills to move from the outdoors in. For some of her residential patrons, such as Ralph and DeWitt Hanes, of Winston-Salem, North Carolina, Shipman worked on both house and garden simultaneously. These Haneses, and others in the region, eventually provided Shipman with a steady and welcome stream of business during troubled years.[2] Her working relationship with the Haneses had an inauspicious beginning, however. DeWitt later recalled, "The night we moved into this great big house was the night of the Crash, and Ralph sat up till dawn." Shipman had visited that spring while the

Pergola garden, Ralph P. Hanes estate, Winston-Salem, N.C., 1929. Photo Shipman office. RMC-Cornell Univ. Library

house was still under construction, "when money was rolling." But, DeWitt pointed out, "she loved Ralph, so she kept coming when the money didn't."[3]

The square garden Shipman designed for the Haneses was reminiscent of her earliest work, an enclosed space structured by four converging paths, a central sundial, and a long Colonial Revival loggia; it was anchored at opposite corners by a brick garden house with dovecote and a white Chippendale-style gate. Beds were given three-dimensional interest with bamboo arches wreathed with the single yellow rose 'Mermaid.' The Haneses affectionately referred to Shipman as "Dim," using her grandchildren's nickname for her. Ralph Hanes once said of Shipman that he had admired her work since he was a college student; she in turn had taught him the therapeutic delights of pruning. Mrs. Hanes remembered Shipman's interest in their ideas: "Before she did any work she sat down with us and said, 'Now you must both tell me your favorite flowers and what you want from a garden—because if anyone asks you who did it, I've been a complete failure.'"[4]

The same aesthetic sensibilities that served Shipman in the landscape also served her in her interior design work; her responsiveness to color, line, texture, and form guided selection of English creamware as surely as her choice of camellia varieties. Shipman bought from the period's best suppliers—Nancy McClelland, Elinor Merrell, and Scalamandré—and scouted auctions and antique shops regularly. Euphanie Mallison, an interior design specialist, joined Shipman's staff around 1938 and directed much of her work for her most enduring clients, Edgar and Edith Stern.

During the 1930s, Shipman began to lecture widely, her lively presentation and "vivid personality" beguiling audiences throughout the country.[5] Her most popular talk was "Color Combination and Perpetual Bloom," but she also spoke about the design and planting of the small garden—her specialty—illustrating the lecture with slides of the Pruyn, Warren, Daniels, Sales, and Greenough gardens, among her other works. In "The Evolution of a Garden," a lecture she first gave in October 1932 in Winston-Salem, Shipman showed one hundred of slides of her own work. In 1935, she gave a series of lectures at the Cosmopolitan Club in New York and, the same year, spoke to the Junior League of Boston.[6] In 1936, Shipman delivered a series of lectures at Lowthorpe School and returned eight years later for another series on design and construction. She commissioned Harry G. Healy, a New York–based architectural photographer, to make several hundred glass slides of her gardens for these and other lectures. (They are now lost.) Healy apparently liked Shipman's work or, at least, working for her. "I have had the most delightful time in my life visiting the several gardens on the list," he wrote. She was less effusive about his pictures and admonished the photographer for ignoring some of her suggestions for specific vantage points.[7]

The slowdown in business coupled with her considerable financial success during the previous decade may have encouraged Shipman to travel abroad for the first time in her life—at age sixty. A trip to Italy in 1929 was followed by two

Ailie du Chêne, pencil sketch of Ellen Shipman, 1932. Nicholas Angell Collection

The Great Depression and the Lure of Europe   155

others to England in the early 1930s. Shipman used slides from these travels in her lectures "English Wayside Gardens" and "Italian Gardens." None of her thoughts about these trips is recorded save a single mention of Europe preserved in the Garden Note Book, where Shipman remembered an evening glimpse of the garden at Ely Cathedral through a locked gate: "when the enchantment of twilight was abroad...the garden possessed strange mystic beauty."[8] We can only guess the influence such trips would have exerted on Shipman's style had they occurred earlier in her development, as they did for so many other designers of the period. It is ironic that the circumstances that compelled her to draw upon more internal—and, by definition, more American—resources may have led to her developing a more distinctive artistic style than she would have after an aesthetic grounding by the prototypical "grand tour."

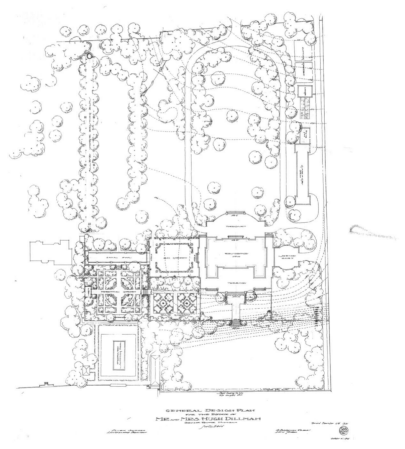

General design plan, Rose Terrace, Hugh Dillman estate, Grosse Pointe, Mich., 2 November 1931. RMC-Cornell Univ. Library

The Gardens of Ellen Biddle Shipman

It is equally ironic that two of Shipman's grandest private commissions, Rose Terrace in Grosse Pointe Farms, Michigan, and Longue Vue in New Orleans—both distinctly of European influence—came to her during the worst years of the Depression. Rose Terrace, an estate on Lake St. Clair, was designed in 1930 by the Philadelphia architect Horace Trumbauer in a late-entry Gilded Age Chateau style.[9] Shipman's clients were Mabel Dodge and Hugh Dillman, a retired actor Dodge had met in Palm Beach, where she owned a splendid oceanfront villa, Playa Riente, designed by the well-known architect Addison Mizner. Dodge may have met Ellen Shipman in Palm Beach, too, as Shipman sometimes overwintered there.

Beginning in 1931, Shipman's office generated nearly one hundred drawings and plans for this complex and, no doubt, lucrative project. Designed in the

Boxwood lawn with statues, Dillman garden, 1931. Photo Preston H. Sweet. RMC-Cornell Univ. Library

Mirror pool, Dillman garden, 1931. Photo Preston H. Sweet. RMC-Cornell Univ. Library

Casino and swimming pool, Dillman garden, 1931. Photo Preston H. Sweet. RMC-Cornell Univ. Library

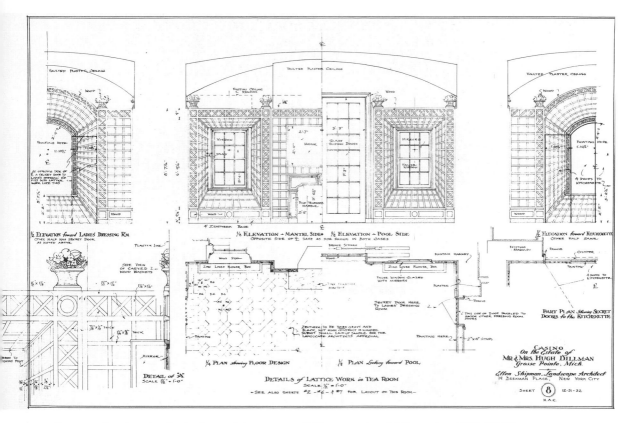

Construction drawing for latticework in tearoom, Dillman garden, 31 December 1932. RMC-Cornell Univ. Library

French style, the garden was something of an anomaly in Shipman's oeuvre. A wide velvet lawn defined by gravel walks and cushions of boxwood hedges finished in a broad, circular mirror pool. The other end of the lawn was bounded by a "canal pool" and latticework bathing casino. The broad proportions, wide horizontal planes, meticulously edged lawns, and delicate detailing captured the combination of intricacy and grandiosity that lay at the heart of eighteenth-century French landscape design.

Shipman's characteristic expressiveness was missing from the taut design, although the plantings that screened the boxwood garden were a typical rich mix of elm, oak, maple, and more exotic deciduous trees. In the rose garden, standards were choreographed into pristine arrangement against vine-covered arches overlooking the pool and lake beyond. The garden's architectural center-piece was an intricately treillaged casino, a far cry from the servicable fieldstone toolhouse Shipman had designed for the Cooper garden nearly twenty years before, although it performed a parallel role in the spatial organization of the garden. Like the toolhouse, it also was multifunctional—dressing room, tea-

Reflecting pool, Longue Vue, Edgar B. Stern estate, New Orleans, La. Photo Shipman office, November 1937. RMC-Cornell Univ. Library

room, and kitchenette—and, also like the Cooper building, it repeated the style of the main house.

Several of its separate elements were exquisite, but Rose Terrace gave the over-all impression that Shipman was designing with an undigested, still-unfamiliar vocabulary. The client's request for a specific stylistic treatment may have prevented her from pursuing a more intuitive scheme. The site was also was a challenge, and Shipman's spare plantings did little to disguise the banality of the flat expanse, which was characterless except for its view of the lake.

She found greater design success in her next big job, Longue Vue, but here, too, her eagerness to pursue large-scale European motifs and spatial arrangements precluded her more expressive romanticism. For two decades Shipman had settled for commissions tightly circumscribed by small budgets and preexisting designs and had watched her colleagues manage much grander assignments. As her fame increased and new opportunities arose, she may have been impatient to test her talents on a more operatic scale. A comment Shipman wrote on the back of a snapshot of Longue Vue captures her pride in the design: "Frank to say I'm impresssed myself when I look upon this magificance."[10]

The Gardens of Ellen Biddle Shipman

Edith and Edgar Stern first saw Shipman's work in a neighboring garden in 1935. The following year, they hired her to design a new landscape for their own estate, whose Colonial Revival house designed by Moise Goldstein dated to 1923. Shipman's friendship with the Sterns deepened quickly. She became their trusted and much-valued arbiter of landscape, architectural, and artistic taste, precisely as Charles Platt had been for many of his clients. Edith Rosenwald Stern was energetic and wealthy, the daughter of the chief executive and principal shareholder of Sears, Roebuck Company. Her husband, a New Orleans native, was a powerful cotton broker. Both were intrepid liberals. Mr. Stern founded a southern university for African American students; Mrs. Stern founded a progressive nursery school when she judged those available to her children to be of inferior quality. In the 1930s they flouted southern convention and hosted a dinner party for opera singer Marian Anderson. The Sterns were devoted to each other and to Longue Vue, and a memorial plaque to "the godmother of the house" attests to their devotion to Shipman.

Vista from terrace garden to south lawn, camellia allée, and "Grant's Tomb," Longue Vue, 1942. Photo Gottscho-Schleisner. Courtesy Longue Vue House and Gardens

The Great Depression and the Lure of Europe   161

Shipman's initial work for the Sterns was limited strictly to the garden. Her scheme for it included a boxwood parterre adjoining a house portico and beyond that, a camellia allée that traced the lines of the original garden plan and forced a dramatic vista. The camellias were transplanted at unprecedented size, all of them dug from the country outside New Orleans, where they had been "pruned" to tree shape by artistic cows.

Soon after the garden was installed, Shipman suggested a more monumental improvement: a new house. She felt that the existing structure was all wrong, since its long rear facade (where one would normally want most of the garden to be) faced east (where there was little property). Having fallen completely under Shipman's charismatic spell, the Sterns agreed to move the existing house and commissioned David Adler, a well known Chicago-based architect, to design a new residence. But Adler proved an inflexible and uncommunicative aesthetic partner and designed a house many times too large for the Sterns' needs, includ-

Portico terrace garden and south facade, Longue Vue, 1942. Photo Gottscho-Schleisner. Courtesy Longue Vue House and Gardens

Lower Hall at Longue Vue. Photo Gottscho-Schleisner, c. 1947. Courtesy Longue Vue House and Gardens

ing upstairs and downstairs central halls that measured forty by sixty feet. Adler's plan also consumed some of the gardens Shipman had just developed. He was dismissed, and Shipman was invited to assume architectural duties for the new house. Her training had not prepared her for the complexities of the task, however, and she was stymied by a chimney that kept appearing in the center of the drawing-room plans. Shipman introduced the Sterns to William and Geoffrey Platt, who had taken over their father's architectural practice after Charles's death in 1933. Despite the Platts' involvement, Shipman appears to have maintained control over the general development of the house design.[11]

Not surprisingly, strong emphasis was placed on the relation of the interior to the exterior and on the facades, which would furnish a lively background for the gardens. While the house exhibited many characteristics of the Classical Revival style, it also reflected an interesting variety of other influences. The east elevation was based on Shadows-on-the-Teche in New Iberia, Louisiana; the south and west elevations were similar to the Le Charpentier-Beauregard House, a raised cottage (circa 1826) in the Vieux Carre section of New Orleans. The approach view was neo-Palladian. Much more heavily fenestrated than the original, the new house presented ample garden views from every room. Most spectacular was the vista from the drawing room out to the camellia allée and tempietto. Construction on Longue Vue II began in 1939 and continued through 1942.

Shipman stepped into the role of interior designer and produced a series of floor plans and scale maquettes. Detailed letters and long telegrams kept her and her clients in near-constant contact as prospective additions to the furnishings were scouted. One such telegram from "Lady Ellen" (as the Sterns called her) ran: "Saw today to be sold at auction Friday most remarkable music box Plays over fifty tunes Exquisite tone About eight figures in band playing on instruments Would be wonderful in playroom May go quite high as very unique and fine Would you like me to bid on it Hope teapot arrives on time."[12]

"You see," explained Mrs. Stern in a 1977 interview, "we weren't really collectors, Mr. Stern and I, but we bought. Ellen Shipman would do all the leg work, and then we'd come up and say it was beautiful." War conditions and the size of the Sterns' fortune put them at a great advantage. "The world was our

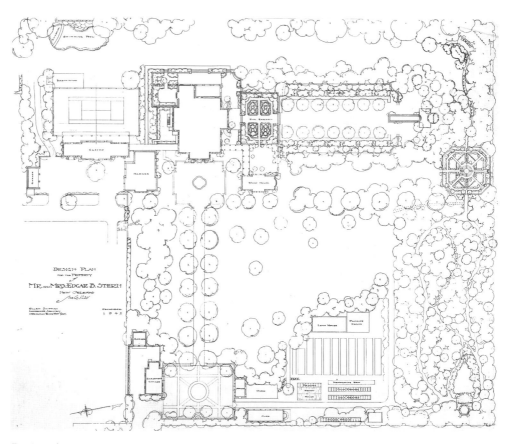

Design plan, Longue Vue II, December 1942. RMC-Cornell Univ. Library

The Gardens of Ellen Biddle Shipman

Azalea walk, Longue Vue, 1942. Photo Gottscho-Schleisner. Courtesy Longue Vue House and Gardens

oyster," continued Edith. "Nobody else was buying. We had the whole market to ourselves."[13]

From their many shopping excursions, Edith Stern particularly remembered Shipman's sharp eye—and her gait. "Ellen Shipman was very tall. She used to walk with these long strides and, so, we went to where they had some garden furniture in the courtyard, bought our bench and, on the way back, she said, 'Did you notice the beautiful pieces of Leeds china on our left, and on our right was a hooked rug I must get for another client.' As far as I could tell, she hadn't seen anything."[14] Shipman's eclectic and practiced eye served her clients well. Their home evolved into a richly textured, warm environment.

Longue Vue's spare garden plan was considerably less cozy, owing to its scale and the monumentality of the major view, bilaterally symmetrical in the French tradition. Thick boundary plantings on three sides kept the eye within the designed landscape. The parterre garden near the south portico was also formal, recalling traditional French prototypes, but Shipman's planting was colorful and inventive. The garden was planted out twice: once for a spring-summer show, a second time in fall. Beyond the long vista, visitors found an informal goldfish pool and seat tucked into the southeast corner of the property and a monumental kitchen garden that combined flowers, fruits, and vegetables in meticulously ordered profusion. Three paths led through the wild garden with its collection of Louisiana iris and other native plants. North of the wild garden were several service gardens and propagating beds.

In 1942, Shipman formalized the approach to the house by creating a long, straight drive and planting a liveoak allée to border it. Courtyard gardens on the north side of the house were added, as were a swimming pool and tennis courts. Shipman's garden survived until 1965, when Hurricane Betsy ripped through New Orleans and destroyed most of the camellia allée.[15]

Longue Vue was one of Ellen Shipman's largest commissions and one of her last residential works. She received an annual retainer of $1,200 ("extras" were carefully scrutinized, however). The thrice-yearly trips she undertook to supervise maintenance and ongoing development of the gardens involved a significant amount of travel—and surely reflected a commitment that transcended pure business. The friendship she developed with Edith and Edgar lasted until she died.

CHAPTER ELEVEN

PUBLIC AND INSTITUTIONAL PROJECTS

IN SEVERAL projects Shipman was able to apply her expressive, romantic idiom to an institutional problem, translating a gardenesque response into a design that held its own on a larger scale while retaining the delicacy and artistic complexity characteristic of her best work. Throughout her career Shipman designed modest planting schemes for schools, libraries, churches, town halls, private clubs, cemetery memorials, and even a railway station.

No single community held more of her public work than Grosse Pointe Shores, where her commissions included the Alger Museum (formerly the Russell Alger home on which she had collaborated with Platt in 1919), a private club, a nurses home, and a convalescent home. In 1932 Shipman also designed a public planting for Lake Shore Drive, which stretched five miles along Lake St. Clair, "kept principally to evergreens [and] willows for early light green—flowering trees and shrubs, especially flowering crabs and plums."[1] The designer's palette represented a divergence from the generic elm and maple street-tree plantings common during the period and may have been influenced by the Prairie Landscape style.

One of Shipman's first recorded public works, the Women's Advisory Council Border for the New York Botanical Garden, came to her in 1928. She approached the design of the 254-foot border as a residential feature, adjusting the scale of

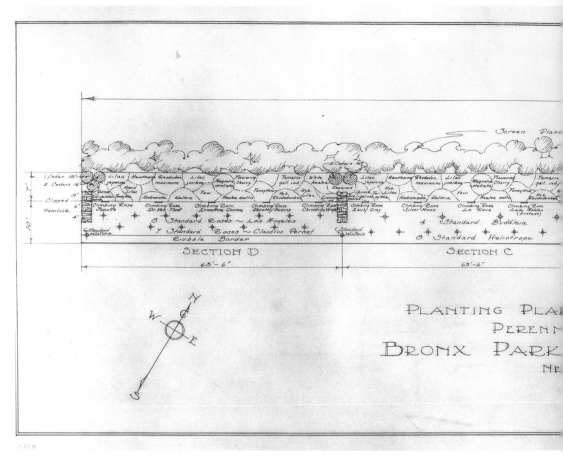

Planting plan for trees and shrubs, Women's Advisory Council border, New York Botanical Garden, Bronx, N.Y., ink on trace, c. 1928. RMC-Cornell Univ. Library

the plantings upward so that the overall proportions and rhythms would not be overwhelmed by the expanse of lawns and big trees nearby. Backed by a screen planting of arborvitae, the border was filled with a mix of flowering shrubs at the rear half and perennials and standards in the front. Shipman was called on to revamp the plantings several times, in 1931, 1935, 1938, and 1946.

During the 1930s, Shipman acquired more prominent public commissions, such as the Fine Arts Center in Colorado Springs, Colorado, in 1935. She had begun the decade with an even grander job for the Aetna Life and Casualty Insurance Company in Hartford, Connecticut. "America's largest Colonial-style office building," designed by the Beaux Arts architect James Gamble Rogers, required planning and planting for a twenty-two-acre site. Almost fifty plans and drawings detail Shipman's work there: wide, tree-studded lawns, formal courts, a roof garden, and decorative details such as a zodiac compass in the forecourt

The Gardens of Ellen Biddle Shipman

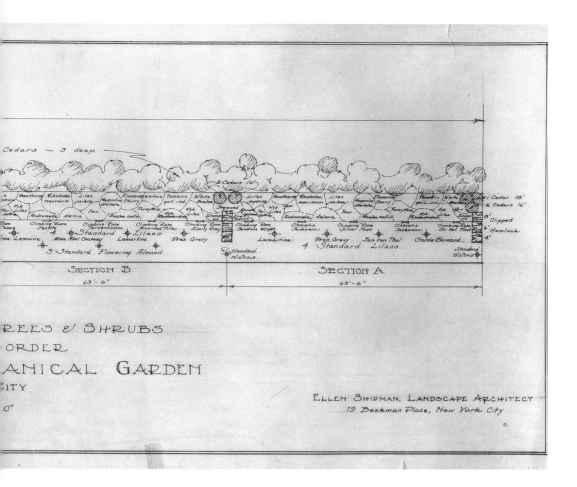

Cedars ~ 3 deep

2 Cedars 16'

SECTION B
63'-6"

SECTION A
63'-6"

REES & SHRUBS
ORDER
ANICAL GARDEN
ITY
O"

ELLEN SHIPMAN, LANDSCAPE ARCHITECT
19 Beekman Place, New York City

paving, the building cornerstone inscription, and specifications for street lamps. The company's president, Morgan B. Brainard, was also a private client; Shipman's work for Aetna likely followed her design for his residence.

Shipman's Olmstedian plan utilized many trees already growing on the former private estates that Aetna's site comprised—one newspaper article recorded over four hundred in thirty species. In addition, twenty-eight elms were to be planted in two L-shaped groups to border the street and line the main walk, many new trees were specified for the lawn, and groups of Korean cherry and flowering crabs were to flank the two circular drives to the front entrance.

Several small gardens added color to the sprawling lawns, and two enclosed courts provided backdrops for the company's cafeterias. More original than any of these features, however, was the private eighth-floor roof garden adjacent to the president's office. Engineered with an extensive drainage system and waterproof concrete floor to hold six feet of soil, the roof garden was surrounded by a

Women's Advisory Council border, 1928. RMC-Cornell Univ. Library

five-foot brick wall that merged with a balustrade supporting large cast-stone urns silhouetted against the Hartford skyline. Shipman's planting included perennials, flowering shrubs, vines, and small trees, such as Korean cherry, magnolia, and plum. The intimate design was a response to the compressed scale of the roof, but it also reflected Shipman's continued interest in domesticity and privacy. Ellen Shipman had given Morgan B. Brainard a room of his own.[2]

A residential spirit also enlivened Shipman's design for a large formal garden at Duke University, originally conceived by her friend Dr. Frederick M. Hanes, an iris fancier and a member of the extended Hanes family for whom she had previously done so much work. Shipman's charge in 1936 was to revamp an ailing iris garden designed a few years before by John C. Wister, a Philadelphia landscape architect. Construction was under way by summer 1937, with costs underwritten by Mary Duke Biddle, a distant relation by marriage to Shipman and daughter of Sarah P. Duke, for whom the gardens were named. Shipman's 10-percent fee, which totaled $4,217, was modest in comparison with the $12,000 annual maintenance cost.[3]

Shipman's new design featured seven curved terraces cradling Japanese cherries, crabapples, and perennial and shrub plantings in a lush presentation of color and texture. ("The slanting light of morning and evening still ignites the beautiful pink-tinted flagstone," wrote one appreciative visitor in 1989.)[4] The main axis extended from a wisteria-covered pergola to a pond at the bottom, the descent along the central path varied by small pools at each level.[5] Again, Shipman made the leap from private to public project without sacrificing the look and feel of a real garden.

Her success in these public jobs raises questions about why Shipman did not do more of them. She apparently did try to find similar commissions, but a variety of circumstances, including stiff competition from her professional colleagues who were also short of work, undermined her efforts. She wrote a long letter of inquiry to the Foundation to Honor Atlanta's War Veterans about a proposed memorial in 1945, in which she cited other public commissions and all her southern references, but little seems to have come of the effort.[6] Shipman's

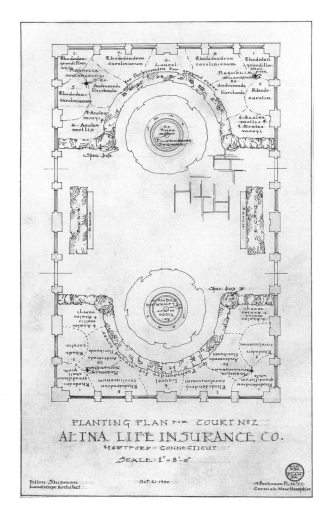

Planting plan for Court No. 2, Aetna Life, Hartford, Conn., ink on trace, 21 October 1930. RMC-Cornell Univ. Library

Roof garden, Aetna Life. Photo Fred Jones, 1931. Courtesy Aetna Life and Casualty

Sarah P. Duke Gardens, Durham, N.C., under construction, February 1938. Duke University Archives

landscape work would always have to be limited to those projects that did not involve large-scale site planning, grading, or natural-resource management, as her short apprenticeship with Platt had not trained her in these specialized tasks. City, campus, subdivision, and park planning, roadway design, and even large estate planning were all beyond her technical grasp. (Platt's abilities in these areas were also limited; he always collaborated with landscape architectural consultants for his public work.) In this regard Shipman differed from her female colleagues Marian Coffin, Marjorie Sewell Cautley, Martha Brookes Hutcheson, Beatrix Farrand, and a few others who acquired the skills and authority necessary not only to design significant public work but to supervise the male crews charged with constructing it.

Sarah P. Duke Gardens, 1940s. Duke University Archives

CHAPTER TWELVE

LAST YEARS

ELLEN SHIPMAN got behind the war effort by offering an intensive eight-week course for women in engineering and drafting skills. She also wanted to share her expertise with the U.S. Army camouflage division, but they declined her services. Not unexpectedly, she became an ardent proponent of victory gardens and proposed that the Garden Club of America use her New York office as a source of information. "Why, I even ... conferred in Washington with the government about the best ways and means of putting across the message of victory gardens," she later wrote. In one lecture, Shipman warned her audience that "anybody who has a spot of ground suitable for raising vegetables and fails to do so is a slacker."[1]

Shipman had almost no work during the war aside from a few interior design commissions, and her business was running in the red. When the war ended, the resumption of her (or anyone else's) specialized, residential practice did not look promising. Labor and materials were in short supply; lifestyles had changed dramatically. Shipman wrote many letters seeking new work and lining up visits to long-standing clients, but they did not yield substantial business. Her office records list twenty-three active clients in 1945, including four in Winston-Salem, four in Perrysville, Ohio, and seven in the surburban New York area. To her Brook Place caretaker, Charles Meyette, Shipman observed, "I do not believe that any other profession has been harder hit than landscape architecture."[2] She borrowed money to keep the office open and reduced her staff to four. She no longer paid herself a salary. Pressed to meet mortgage payments on the Beekman Place property, Shipman cashed in some of her stocks and bonds. In October 1946, she reluctantly sold her New York residence, office, and furnishings to

Edith and Edgar Stern. She had been leasing out the apartments there for several years, living instead at the Beekman Towers Hotel around the corner.

The summer after the war ended, Shipman reopened Brook Place, which had been closed since 1941. Meyette aired the house and cleaned up the garden. Shipman found a student to help in the garden, drive the car, draft, and type. The day-to-day routine was reminiscent of earlier years, but simpler. Guests were invited to lunch prepared and served by two students from the Cornell home economics school or to a light supper followed by one of Mrs. Meyette's pies. Shipman looked after the needs and expenses of her staff, and saw to it that they were treated to the movies once a week. Dona E. Caldwell, who worked for Shipman that summer, remembers that duties were light and her boss was "kind, gentle, and often protested that I should not work so hard."[3]

In 1945, another employee, Anne Bruce Haldeman, helped Shipman prepare a book outlining her design philosophies. Haldeman was a graduate of the Cambridge School and had worked in the office during the last few years.[4] The Garden Note Book, however, was never finished owing to the vagaries of the postwar market for gardening books and Shipman's increasingly ill health. William Platt's introduction, if ever realized, has never surfaced.[5] Shipman's text was aimed at the home gardener in a congenial how-to tone, suggesting that she viewed it not as a vehicle for her theoretical legacy but rather as an attempt to inspire would-be gardeners. She expressed the hope that the reader would "grow to be a great and enthusiastic gardener bringing joy and happiness to yourself, your family and your community." The impassioned prose was inspired by Shipman's own excitement for her art: "Even writing of the planning of these simple beginnings is exciting—the real experience of learning to start and grow your own plants is the thrill of a lifetime." Shipman's text also reflected her view that gardening was not only the most civilized of arts but also the most democratic: "all mankind can walk through, rich and poor, high and low, talented and untalented. It has no distinctions, all are welcome."[6]

Shipman may have planned to incorporate selections from her Blue Books into the completed publication. These well-worn looseleaf notebooks contained a hodgepodge of *Country Life* news clippings, notes on lectures, nursery lists, client plant lists, recommended plant combinations, regional plant lists, and other horticultural information, which she shared with clients and other designers. Shipman may have imagined that a book would boost her flagging business or supplement her dwindling income, but it is likely that postwar homeowners, most of them more interested in barbecues than ornamental pools, would have found some of the ideas proposed in the text old-fashioned.

In 1946, Shipman received a letter from the architect Aymar Embury inviting her to become a member of the Institute of Arts and Letters. It would have been the only professional recognition she received during her career. She declined Embury's offer, suggesting that he look for someone younger, "to whom it might make a great difference." Shipman continued, "I know what it would have meant to me fifteen or twenty years ago, but now, soon perhaps, I shall not be working."[7] Shipman had never actively sought professional affiliation or joined her own field's professional organization, the American Society of Landscape Architects. When, after Shipman's death, her assistant Frances McCormic was asked the reason, she reported that her boss "didn't approve of it," she was "too busy," and found the people "dull."[8] All these explanations are plausible, but none speaks to the profound disparity between Shipman's goals and those of the ASLA.

For its first twenty-five years, the ASLA was run almost as a men's club, not only sexist but geographically chauvinistic. "If one were not a white, male, eastern college graduate," writes historian Diane Kostial McGuire, "the atmosphere was quite chilly."[9] Eager to secure a place for the new profession in relation to its older, well-established rivals, engineering and architecture, the predominantly male organization deemphasized gardens and residential work in favor of larger, public-scale work. The vast majority of Shipman's commissions, of course, were of the former category. The network that provided Shipman with most of her clients, speaking engagements, and other professional opportunities was founded and run by women: the Garden Club of America. Their client-centered emphasis on horticulture, aesthetics, taste, community service, and the environment more clearly resembled her own.

Early in 1947, at age seventy-eight, Shipman closed her office for good. Recurring bouts of pneumonia had forced her to curtail the annual garden visits that constituted the greater part of her practice. On her doctor's advice, she reluctantly decided to refuse new work. But she had not anticipated the sense of loss she would suffer in leaving her practice. "Closing the office was much harder in *every* way than I had realized it would be," she wrote Edith Stern. "I have been through so many things in my long years—that I thought this would be nothing! But when it came to having to go through literally thousands of plans and deciding what to destroy and what to keep, and each one bringing up the past and the realization of the work that was put into them and the joys—and so many of them all gone—owing to the depression and the war." Shipman's letter continued on a happier note: she no longer had her work, but she would keep, until the end, the other source of joy in her life, her family. "I am here at Brook Place and Ellen and the children are with me for two weeks. Simply heaven. I forget the work that I must do and just rejoice in the beauty and blessed family life."[10]

With her elder daughter and her family, Shipman found a deeply satisfying domestic stability that had eluded her as a young mother. She had a close rela-

View from terrace, Ease House, Warwick West, Bermuda, late 1930s or early 1940s. Nancy Angell Streeter Collection

tionship with her grandchildren and her son-in-law, Montgomery Angell, who was also her financial adviser. The Angells visited Shipman in Brook Place, Beekman Place, and at her winter home in Bermuda. And Shipman was a frequent visitor to their home, High House, in Garrison, New York.

Shipman's contacts with her two younger children were less frequent. Evan and Mary, however, were close and continued to share an interest in horses. Mary trained horses in Virginia, where her clients included the Whitneys and duPonts; her first husband, Cary Jackson, owned a country store.[11] Evan, who struggled with alcoholism, eventually gave up writing poetry to turn his attention to a harness-racing column for the *Morning Telegraph.*

During her final years, Shipman spent more and more time in Warwick West, Bermuda, where she had purchased a piece of land from which she could see both sides of the island and designed "the nicest house in the world," with gardens down the south slope.[12] After celebrating her eightieth birthday in November 1949 with her family in New York, Shipman returned to Ease House for the winter. At the end of February 1950, she wrote excitedly to Edith Stern about an anticipated visit from her grandchildren and an upcoming Garden Club of America meeting in Grosse Pointe Shores. She expressed great pride in her designs there and a strong desire that Edith make the trip north. "I do hope [you go] because you will see more of my work in one place than in any other ten places.... I know of six [gardens] to be shown." Shipman said she intended to be there, too, and closed on an intimate note: "I have to limit myself to one sheet [of stationery] but that does not limit the amount of love I send you each and all."[13]

On March 27, four days after the Angells were to arrive in Bermuda, Ellen Shipman died of pneumonia at Ease House. By then, most of the six hundred gardens she had designed during her lifetime had changed beyond recognition. Many were simply gone, and her work was quickly forgotten. Ellen Shipman's talent—an extraordinary talent—had escaped documentation in the annals of American landscape history.

All gardens are vulnerable to the vagaries of their owners' whims and the inevitable growth and decay of plants, but Ellen Shipman's were particularly fragile in this respect. Had she pursued more monumental designs, she would have left behind a more tangible mark. Her responsiveness to place and to the wishes of her clients led her to create gardens whose sensuality and delicacy depended on an evanescence that made their eclipse almost inevitable.

Ellen Biddle Shipman on her eightieth birthday, November 1949.
Plainfield Historical Society

EPILOGUE

ELLEN SHIPMAN'S family diligently carried out her wishes regarding the disposition of her professional effects. Shipman requested that the executors "set aside such of my books, plans and photographs as seem to them to have been pertinent to my work in my profession and to give ... [them] to one of the following institutions: (a) Vassar College; (b) Cornell University; (c) Cambridge School of Landscape Architecture; and (d) New York Public Library." Cornell University accepted the gift in 1953. Shipman left her slide collection to the Garden Club of America, although its whereabouts is unknown today. Some of her professional books were donated to the Avery Architectural Library at Columbia University, where Charles Platt's extensive archives were placed.[1] In 1946, about the time that she drew up her will, Shipman offered copies of plans for southern projects to the Department of Landscape Architecture at the University of Georgia; although the offer was enthusiastically accepted, there is no record that the gift was ever made.[2]

AFTERWORD

The Restoration of the English Garden at Stan Hywet

John Franklin Miller

THE STORY OF Stan Hywet begins in 1911, when Warren Manning first surveyed the property and reported to his clients, F. A. and Gertrude Seiberling, that "very few of the thousand or more properties" he had "examined and made plans for offer within a hundred acres so many and such varied incidents that will give a home estate distinction and interest." Manning's design was centered on a wild garden that maximized the property's existing features, but his collaboration with architect Charles Schneider resulted in the design of more formal garden areas—allées, terraces, and enclosed garden rooms. One of these, the English Garden, was Mrs. Seiberling's favorite retreat.

According to family tradition, the walled, screened, and partially sunken English Garden was inspired by Frances Hodgson Burnett's book *The Secret Garden,* published in 1912 just as plans for Stan Hywet were being formulated. Like its fictional counterpart, Stan Hywet's English Garden was a private enclosure, hidden from view by evergreens and shrubs, filled with luxuriant plantings of sun-loving flowers. Mrs. Seiberling used it as a place of refuge, for reflection, inspiration, and rejuvenation.

Manning paid a final visit to Stan Hywet in 1928, at which time Mrs. Seiberling, a talented painter, may have requested a new horticultural plan for her secret garden, one that used a lighter palette of color and greater variety of flowering plants. Rather than undertake the design himself, Manning suggested that Ellen Shipman be brought in, describing her to his client as "one of the best, if not the very best, flower garden maker in America." Mrs. Seiberling apparently followed Manning's advice; there are plans from Shipman's office, dated 11 May 1929, in the estate's archives.

Over the years, economic adversity led to the gradual decline in the maintenance of the estate, which accelerated with Mrs. Seiberling's death in 1946. After Mr. Seiberling died in 1955, a private organization of community volunteers negotiated with family donors to preserve, maintain, and operate the property for public benefit. During the early period of this stewardship, however, energy and enthusiasm were not focused on accuracy or authenticity in the gardens. Alterations were made to the property to attract visitors, and new plants were introduced which changed the original design intent. Maintenance of the English Garden was assumed by the Akron Garden Club, who replanted it in the sixties and seventies. By 1985, the area had developed into a shade garden tucked away in a grove of now-towering evergreens and deciduous trees. It was a charming and serene retreat, but most of the original plantings had long since disappeared and the architectural fabric of the garden had deteriorated significantly.

In 1989, the Stan Hywet Hall Foundation commissioned a firm of consulting architects to advise on the restoration of the English Garden and the adjoining West Terrace. Their report recommended the complete rehabilitation of the garden's Arts and Crafts–style architecture. But the question arose, could such rehabilitation be accomplished without sacrificing a majority of the existing plants?

Another question came up as well: which of the very different English Gardens that had existed on the site should be restored—the original design created by Manning's office soon after 1915, the planting of 1929–30 following Ellen Shipman's plan, or the garden planted by the Akron Garden Club after 1957? Stan Hywet's archives documented all three.

In the 1970s, Stan Hywet's board of trustees had approved a policy establishing the years 1915 to 1930 as the period of greatest historical and artistic significance in the house; in 1986, the board confirmed that the same time frame should apply to garden restorations. According to that criterion, the Garden Club creation, since it did not reflect the critical 1915–30 period, could not be considered (nor did that garden as it appeared in the 1970s and 1980s reflect the original design intent). Manning's garden was documented by photographs showing family members in it in the early twenties, but no plans or other evidence, except his rudimentary plant list indicating color schemes, survived to enable accurate and confident restoration of the garden of this era. The Shipman plan of 1929, by contrast, provided precise locations for more than 3,400 plants representing at least 112 different varieties of perennials and bulbs. As they reviewed the possibilities, Stan Hywet's stewards realized that they had to choose between a highly conjectural restoration of the Manning-era garden of 1918–29 and a horticulturally precise restoration based on the Shipman plans of 1929. The board-established Garden Landscape Committee conducted a review process.

The choice was not so simple as it might appear. Members of the Seiberling family had fond memories of the Manning garden, and individually they stated reservations about whether Shipman's plans had ever been carried out. But slides and photographs began to surface in archival and family collections which confirmed that the principal features of Mrs. Shipman's plans had been implemented in 1929–30 and maintained in some fashion for the next twenty-five years. Still, the final decision of which design to restore hinged on the decisions to proceed with the costly architectural renovation (the need for which had been confirmed) and to cut down the surrounding shade-giving trees (a report on light conditions had concluded that restoration of Shipman's plan required their removal).

A campaign to foster support for the Shipman plan was begun. Advocates stressed the growing importance of authentic garden restoration and interpretation and the distinction of Ellen Shipman in twentieth-century American garden design history. They also recalled the intent of the original family donors, expressed in the mandate of the seventies, to preserve Stan Hywet's artistic character. It was acknowledged that one of the long-term benefits of a restoration to the Shipman plan would be increased recognition of Stan Hywet's leadership role in garden restoration work to the highest obtainable standards.

However, resistance to the idea of altering the character of the English Garden continued and needed to be addressed. Some people felt that sacrifice of the existing plants would be a wasteful loss; others believed that it would be difficult for staff to maintain the Shipman plan. Without the increased understanding of Ellen Shipman's role in twentieth-century garden design, it is unlikely that the project would have been launched. Warren Manning's endorsement was high praise, indeed, and there was ever-broader recognition of her accomplishments coast to coast and especially in northeast Ohio. As interest in Shipman's record of work grew, it became easier to convince people of the advisability of proceeding with restoration of the only flower garden at Stan Hywet for which there existed a precise horticultural plan.

In 1989, the Akron Garden Club voted a pledge of $155,000 in support of the garden's complete architectural and horticultural restoration, and their generosity was matched by grants from the Helen S. Wolle Trust and the John S. Knight Foundation. A project plan was formulated and the restoration was begun.

After additional surveys and assessments, a color study, and preparation of research data on historical plants, actual work got under way in 1991. New drainage and irrigation systems were installed; pools rebuilt; walls, walks, and steps repaired; and restoration done on woodwork and wrought iron door hardware. Excavation of new drainage trenches during the "demolition phase" was shocking to many people and unsettling even to the most committed. Discovery

of a vertical fissure in Willard Paddock's statue *The Garden of the Water Goddess,* which was a focal point of the garden, caused a major setback. After a conservator evaluated the sculpture, it was determined that the fissure should be repaired, the interior properly plumbed, and the surface repatinated—expenses that had not been figured into the original budget.

While the architectural restoration proceeded, removal of the trees outside the garden generated alarmingly large stacks of logs. Stan Hywet's garden staff distracted itself by working closely with horticultural restoration consultants to confirm descriptions and sources for the trees, shrubs, perennials, bulbs, and vines needed to create the Shipman planting scheme. The summer of 1991 was devoted to a search for the 107 varieties of plants Ellen Shipman specified, following the master list developed by Stan Hywet's horticultural consultant. Stan Hywet's horticultural staff contacted twenty-six nurseries and plant suppliers across the country, eventually acquiring all but a few plants, which could not be located and for which no acceptable substitutes could be found.

With great anticipation, the staff began replanting in the autumn of 1991, but they soon encountered an annoying obstacle: the contractors who had rebuilt the pools and reset the walks had neglected to remove excess concrete below the soil surface; planting was impossible. A landscape contractor was called in with concrete saws to remove unwanted masonry.

When trees, shrubs, and the first herbaceous plants were in place, Ellen Shipman's genius in structuring visual interest was revealed. Pools and the fountain statue on the north-south axis balanced the exuberant flowering borders around the perimeter walls. Trees and shrubs marked strategic points in evergreen areas. Full-scale replanting of perennials, biennials, and vines followed, utilizing a template and intricate placement system devised by horticultural consultants.

In 1992, Irene Seiberling Harrison, the 102-year-old daughter of the garden's original patron, cut the ribbon, officially opening her mother's restored English Garden to the public.

After several growing seasons, the English Garden continues to provide valuable lessons in the restoration maintenance of historic gardens. Weather conditions make it impossible to predict accurately which plants may need to be replaced, and sometimes plants needed to maintain the design cannot be ordered in time. Deadheading, tidying up the beds and walks after heavy public use, and cleaning debris from the pool surfaces provide a never-ending list of chores for staff and volunteers. Furthermore, Shipman's willingness to allow lush plantings to work against a too-contrived tidiness has led some visitors to question the design intent—and Stan Hywet's maintenance commitment. Not all refinements can be implemented, or at least not immediately. Espaliered pear trees, for example, grow very slowly; it takes several years and advance planning to prepare them for installation. Other issues arise: how much garden furniture should there be? and what if the answer requires the removal of furniture donated in past years in tribute to Garden Club members? How much pruning is required to maintain climbing roses and other vines? Perhaps the single most difficult maintenance issue concerns shrub replacement. A case in point is the yew (*Taxus cuspidata*), which restoration consultants believe Shipman intended to have remain low and loose; as the years passed, however, the yew hedges grew overlarge and were sheared. Should Stan Hywet maintain original design intent or will it be necessary to lengthen cycles for shrub replacement, at some point mandating the shearing of shrubs to replicate their appearance in historic photos? Such are the questions to be resolved as principles for historic garden maintenance evolve.

The magnificent and unique character of the English Garden makes all this labor seem unquestionably worthwhile, and the garden's glory is proof enough that restoration of a Shipman plan is possible and desirable. As the years pass, challenges will continue—there is no doubt of that—but the continuing benefit to visitors and staff will offset the effort required to meet them. As stewards of one of the few preserved Shipman designs anywhere, we are fortunate to have—at last—the larger picture of her work and design philosophy to guide us as we continue to make difficult and exciting preservation decisions.

The Gardens of Ellen Biddle Shipman

APPENDIX

Client List

The basis for this list is an alphabetical roster of over six hundred clients which Frances McCormic drew up in 1945, when Shipman's practice resumed after languishing during the war years. In a separate section McCormic lists twenty-three active clients for 1945, and new names were penciled in until the office closed in 1947. The lack of documentation at Cornell (once thought to have near-complete holdings) for many names on McCormic's list does not necessarily mean that those projects were not carried out. Typically, the clients would have retained their set of plans, which in some cases still exist in private archives. Some of the listed projects were not, in fact, executed: a few clients may have been unable to proceed after engaging Shipman's services, and others may have abandoned a project before working plans were drawn up.

I have cross-checked McCormic's list against holdings at Cornell and at the University of Oregon; from these records, I have added more names (overlooked by McCormic), culling information as well from Shipman's notes and correspondence, and from regional resources. As an aid to future research, I have included other information when available—property name, architect, landscape architect, dates, archives, and published references.

When the client's name is unclear or the location is uncertain or missing, I have given editorial information in brackets. Client names and geographical locations are cited as they appear on plans and letters and may not correspond with current names and locations. I have made every effort to eliminate errors, but I have not been able to verify every entry. For further information refer to the Bibliography.

Client names are arranged alphabetically by state rather than by city, except for "clusters" (Chagrin Falls, Ohio; Greenwich, Conn.; Grosse Pointe, Mich.; Long Island; Mount Kisco, N.Y., and Philadelphia), which can be found at the end of the appropriate state.

Abbreviations

 a architect
 bib see Bibliography for references
 la landscape architect
 * projects illustrated in this book
 AAG Archives of American Gardens (slides)
 CU Ellen Shipman Collection, Cornell University (plans, photographs, correspondence)

Information in entries is arranged as follows:

Client. Property, location, initial date, collaborating architect or landscape architect and dates, archive, references, previous or subsequent owners

Godley, Mrs. George McM. Long House, CU, bib.

Hanley, William L. Jr. Harrie T. Lindeberg (a), 1937, CU

Mahaney, David

Marshall, Hugh B. 1944, CU

McConnell, Albert R. CU

*Mitchell, Mrs. Ormsby. 1929, Alfred Hopkins (a), 1929, CU, bib.

Munroe, Charles

Noble, Mrs. Robert P. 1947, Phelps Barnum (a), Marian Coffin (la), 1930s, CU

Reed, Joseph Verner. 1938, CU

Rockefeller, J. S. 1938, CU

Sargent, John

Satterlee, Herbert L.

Truesdale, Mrs. Melville D. Four Trees, 1945, CU, UO

Vietor, Ernest G.

Walcott, Frederick C.

*Williams, Clark. Live Oak, 1925, CU, bib.

Wood, Mrs. E. Allan. Richard Dana (a), CU, bib., subsequent owner Hugh B. Marshall

Woods, Mrs. Richard A. Hillside Farm, 1946, CU

Yandell, Lundsford P. CU, former Elkanah Mead Homestead

Delaware

Callery, G. L. New Castle, CU

Du Pont. Centerville, CU

Du Pont, E. I. Wilmington, 1928, CU

Du Pont, Ernest. Wilmington, CU

Du Pont, Eugene. Owl's Nest, Greenville, 1928, Harrie T. Lindeberg (a), 1917, AAG, CU

Haskell, Mrs. Harry G. Hill Girt Farm, Wilmington, c. 1928, CU

Hilles, Mrs. William. Wilmington

Willson, Reynolds. Greenville, CU

Florida

Cummer, Arthur. Jacksonville, 1931, CU

West, Mrs. Authur L. Tallahassee, CU

Georgia

Atkinson, H. M. Atlanta, CU

Croly, Mrs. Herbert. St. Simon's Island

Goodrum, J. J. Atlanta

McRae, Floyd. Atlanta

Torrey, Dr. H. H. Savannah

Williams, Joseph A. Cobb County, CU

Illinois

Armour, Lester. Lake Forest

Baird, Clay. Evanston

Blair, William McCormick. Crab Tree Farm, Lake Bluff, CU

Butler, Harmon B. Winnetka

Clow, Mrs. Kent. Lake Forest, Jens Jensen (la), 1910, CU

Douglas, Donald. Lake Forest

Gardner, Mrs. Robert A. Lake Forest, CU

Gross, Alfred. Evanston

Lichtstern, A. J. Highland Park, Jens Jensen (la), 1915

McLennon, Donald. Lake Forest

Niblack, Austin. Lake Forest, Jens Jensen (la), 1914

Reynolds, Arthur. Lake Forest

Shumway, Mrs. Edward. Lake Forest, AAG

Spalding, Mrs. Vaughan. Lake Forest, bib.

Kentucky

Brady, James Cox. Fayette County and Lexington, CU, UO

De Waal, Mrs. Christian. Lexington, CU, bib.

Haggin, Louis. Versailles, 1941, CU

Speed, William S. Kanawha, Louisville, 1917, Charles A. Platt (a), 1917

Louisiana

Garden Study Club. Audubon Park, New Orleans, CU

Lemann, Monte. New Orleans, 1938, CU

*Stern, Edgar B. and Edith. Longue Vue, New Orleans, 1935, Geoffrey Platt (a), 1939, CU, bib., open to the public

Williams, Mrs. Charles S. New Orleans, 1934, CU

Williams, Mrs. Frank. New Orleans

Williams, Laurence K. New Orleans, CU

Maine

Alger, Mrs. Russell A. Jr. York Harbor, 1926, CU, bib.

Allen, Seabury. York Harbor, 1920s
Allen, Mrs. Seabury. Kittery Point, 1941, CU
Austin, Edith. Kittery
Lewis, Mrs. Howard W. York Harbor, 1945,
    CU; York Village, 1944
Mellon, Mrs. M. T. Northeast Harbor,
    1945, CU
*Parsons, Llewellyn. Kennebunk, 1914, Olm-
    sted Bros. (la), 1910, Arthur Shurtleff (la),
    1916, Fletcher Steele (la), 1945, CU, DC,
    now a part of Rachel Carson National
    Seashore

Maryland

Baker, William. Baltimore County, CU
Conoley, Douglas. Tulip Hill, Cumberstone,
    1945, CU
Fay, Col. W. G. Leonardstown, CU
Hale, Chandler. Upper Marlboro
Welles, Sumner. Oxon Hill, UO

Massachusetts

Abbott, Gordon Abbott. Glass Head, Man-
    chester, c. 1921, bib.
Ames, Mrs. Hobart. North Easton, Fletcher
    Steele (la), 1931
Ames, John. North Easton, CU
Austin, Edith. Marion
Bemis, Frank. Beverly Farms; Boston, CU
Bradley, Mrs. Gardner. Wellesley, CU
Bradley, Robert. Prides Crossing
Bullock, Calvin. Royalston
Charles River Square. Boston
Converse, C. C. Magnolia
Crocker, Douglas. Fitchburg, CU
*Daniels, Mrs. Alanson L. Old Farm, Wenham,
    1913, CU
DeBlois, Mrs. George L. Ipswich, 1918, DC
Elliot, Dr. John. Dedham
Emmons, Mrs. Robert W. Monument Beach,
    1924, CU
Fessenden, Russell G. Concord, 1920,
    CU, DC
Frothingham, Mrs. Louis. North Easton, Her-
    bert J. Kellaway (la), CU
Green, Albert. Belmont

*Greenough, Mrs. Henry V. Brookline, 1925,
    CU, bib.
Hanna, D. R. Lenox
Harris, Mrs. Julian Hartwell. Nantucket,
    1930, CU
Harrower, Mrs. Norman. Fitchburg, 1931
Herter, Christian A. Millis, 1935, CU
Houghton, Arthur A. South Dartmouth,
    1937, CU
Johnson, Wolcott H. South Hamilton
Kent, Edward L. Prides Crossing
King, Frederick P. Manchester, 1942, CU
Leland, Lester. Manchester
Lewis, George Jr. Sherborn, CU
Longfellow, Alice. Cambridge, 1925, Martha
    Brookes Hutcheson (la), 1904, and more
    recent work, now Longfellow National
    Historic Site, open to the public
Lowthorpe School. Groton, 1942, CU
*McGinley, Mrs. Holden. Milton, 1925,
    Winslow & Bigelow (a), CU, UO, bib.
Milton Bird Sanctuary. Milton
Parker, William A. North Easton, CU
Proctor, Mrs. Rodney. Stockbridge, 1936, CU
Putnam, Mrs. George. Manchester, 1936,
    Fletcher Steele (la), 1953, CU
Sedgwick, Mrs. Ellery (Mabel Cabot). Long
    Hill, Beverly, 1930, CU, owned by The
    Trustees of Reservations, open to the public
Spalding, Philip L. Spalding, Marion, Fletcher
    Steele (la), 1924, CU
Spaulding, S. S. Springfield, CU
Warren, Bayard. Prides Crossing
*Warren, Mrs. Samuel D. Bohemia Manor,
    Mattapoisett, 1912, CU
Warren, Sylvia. Dover, CU
Watson, Gertrude. Pittsfield
West, Thomas. Woods Hole
Whittier, Albert R. Milton, CU

Michigan (see also Grosse Pointe)

Brown, Mrs. Joseph E. Kalamazoo, 1919, DC
Campbell, H. M. Detroit, CU
*Ford, Henry and Clara. Fair Lane, Dearborn,
    1927, Jens Jensen (la), Herbert J. Kellaway
    (la), CU, now part of University of Michigan

Greening Nurseries. Munroe, CU

Harris, William. Detroit

Hudson, Judge Robert P. Sault Sainte Marie, CU

Hull, Blanche. Kalamazoo

King, Mrs. Francis. Orchard House, Alma, c. 1923, CU

*Lowe, Edward. Holmdene, Grand Rapids, 1921, Winslow & Bigelow (a), Ossian C. Simonds (la), CU, bib.

Mount Clemens Convalescent Home. Mount Clemens

Remick, Jerome. Detroit

Rust, A. M. Saginaw, CU

*Smith, Angus. Detroit, 1928, CU

Smith, Henry B. Bay City, 1927, CU

Smith, Hubert. Bay City, CU

Talbot, Mrs. George. Saginaw, 1937, CU

Grosse Pointe

Alger, Mrs. Frederick M. 1928, CU

*Alger, Russell A. Jr. and Marion. The Moorings, 1917, Charles A. Platt (a), 1908, AAG, CU, bib., renamed Alger Museum 1937, now Grosse Pointe War Memorial, open to the public

Alger, Mrs. Russell A. 1930, William Platt (a), CU

Allington, Mrs. Courtenay D. 1930, AAG, CU

Altland, Daniel

*Barbour, Mrs. Edwin Scott (Edith). Longue Vue, 1927, CU, bib.

Bowen, Julian. Wallace Frost (a), 1927

Bryant, John

Bulkley, Leavitt

Campbell, Mrs. H. M. CU

Chapin, Roy D and Inez. 1946, Bryant Fleming (a), Fletcher Steele (la), 1954

Corbett, Valeria

*Dillman, Hugh and Mabel Dodge. Rose Terrace, 1931, Horace Trumbauer (a), 1930, CU, bib.

Dyar, Mrs. John

Edwards, Allen F. Charles A. Platt (a), 1927

Ferry, Mrs. Dexter M. Trowbridge & Ackerman (a), 1915, CU

Grosse Pointe Club. Robert O. Derrick (a), 1927

Grosse Pointe Nurses Home

Harris, Julian Hartwell. William B. Stratton (a), 1924, CU

Jackson, Roscoe. c. 1933

Kanzler, Ernest. 1947, Bryant Fleming (a), CU, bib.

Lake Shore Drive. 1932, CU

Lee Gate Subdivision. CU

Longyear, Mrs. Howard

Lord, Herbert

Lord, John N. CU

MacCrone, Ed

McGraw, Mrs. Arthur. Charles A. Platt (a), 1926

McGraw, Mrs. Theodore Jr. 1922, Alfred Hopkins (a), CU, bib.

McNaughton, Lynn. CU

Mendelsonn, Louis. CU

Miller, Sidney Jr.

Murphy, Blanche Murphy

Murphy, Dr. Frederick T. c. 1933, CU

Newberry, Mrs. John S. Jr. Lone Hill Farm, c. 1928, Albert Kahn (a), 1911, AAG, CU, bib.

Newberry, Mrs. Truman H. Trowbridge & Ackerman (a), William Pitkin (la)

Pittman, Stuart

Sales, Carter

*Sales, Mrs. Murray W. 1927, Louis Kamper (a), 1917, CU, bib.

Schlotman, Joseph B. c. 1929, Albert H. Sparh (a), 1915, CU, des.

Shelden, Henry D. UO

Smith, Howard. 1928, CU

Stephens, Mrs. Henry. 1917, Charles A. Platt (a), 1913, CU

Stevens, William P. 1929, CU

Webber, Oscar. 1928, CU

Webber, Richard

New Hampshire

Bane [Baynes?] Memorial [Ernest Harold Baynes, founder of Meriden Bird Club, died 1925]. Meriden

Drake, Joshua. CU

Dyer, Lyman T. Orford, CU

Goodyear, A. Conger. High Court, Cornish, 1914, Charles A. Platt (a), 1890, CU, previous owners Annie Lazarus and Norman Hapgood

Griffith, Theodore B. Thimble Farm, Little Boar's Head, Rye, c. 1920, CU

Hill, Albert E. Plainfield

Meriden Bird Club. Meriden

Philip Read Memorial Library, Plainfield

Plainfield School. Plainfield, c. 1929, plan at Philip Read Memorial Library, Plainfield

Saint-Gaudens Memorial. Cornish, 1928, CU, bib., now Saint-Gaudens National Historic Site, open to the public

New Jersey

Augustus, Ellsworth. Orange

Beinecke, Frederick W. Madison

Bliss, Mrs. Walter P. Bernardsville, CU

Brady, James Cox. Hamilton Farms, Gladstone, 1925, CU, now Olympic Equestrian Training Center

Brown, J. Wright. Red Bank

Brown, William C. Short Hills

Castles, J. W. Convent

Colgate, Henry. Morristown

Cutting, C. Suydam. Gladstone, early 1930s, bib.

Dane, William. Llewellyn Park

Edison, Mrs. Thomas A. (Mina). Glenmont, Llewellyn Park, 1926, Ernest Bowditch (la), 1907, now Edison National Historic Site, open to the public

Farish, William

Foster, F. Vernon. Peapack, Edmund T. See (a), 1930s, bib.

Fowler, Anderson A. Peapack, Mott B. Schmidt (a), 1925

Franks, Mrs. Robert A. Bonaire, Llewellyn Park, 1920s, AAG, CU, bib.

Gambrill, Richard. Peapack

Geddes, Susan C. Montclair

Hanks, George J. Orange, 1940, CU

Hersloff, Nils B. Llewellyn Park

Hodson, Mrs. C. Orange, 1941, CU

Hopkins, Alfred. Princeton, 1932, Alfred Hopkins (a), bib.

Kinnicutt, Mrs. G. Herman. Far Hills, Marian Coffin (la), CU

Martin, Emma. Princeton, 1938, CU

Mathews, Rev. Paul. Princeton

Metcalf, Manton B. Rumson

Mettler, John W. East Millstone

Moseley, Mrs. Fred S. Far Hills, CU

Prentice, John H. Willow Brook, Bernardsville, CU

Ratliff, Mrs. R. Stockton, 1941, CU

Reeves, Mrs. Richard Early. Summit, 1924, Calvert Vaux (la for former owner), 1889, Carl A. Pilat (la), 1924, bib., now Reeves-Reed Arboretum, open to the public

Rutherfurd, Winthrop. Allamuchy

Schiff, Jacob. Seabright, c. 1926, James L. Greenleaf (la), CU

*Schley, Evander B. Far Hills, 1924, Peabody, Wilson & Brown (a), CU, UO, bib., now part of Moreland Farms

Schley, Reeve. Far Hills, CU

Smillie, Ralph. Essex Fells, 1943, CU

Stillwell, Dr. Edward C. Essex Fells, 1945, CU

Terry, Willis. Bernardsville

Vanderpool, Wynant D. Morristown

Vietor, John A. Seabright, CU

Weston, Edward. Montclair, CU

New Mexico

Proctor, F. Santa Fe, CU

New York (see Long Island: Nassau County, Long Island: Suffolk County, Mount Kisco, New York City, Suburban New York, Upstate and Western New York State)

Long Island: Nassau County

Bacon, Mrs. Robert L. Old Acres, Westbury, 1920s, bib.

Belmont, August. Syosset

Burchard, Anson. Locust Valley

Bushnell, Leslie. Oyster Bay

Clarke, J. Averell. Westbury, 1927, Peabody, Wilson & Brown (a), 1920, CU, SPLIA

Cushman, Paul. Syosset, UO

Davis, Arthur. Mill Neck

Davis, John W. Locust Valley

Dyer, George R. Roslyn, Charles A. Platt (a), 1909

Emmet, Richard S. High Elms, Glen Cove, c. 1929, Peabody, Wilson & Brown (a), SPLIA

Gossler, Philip. Topsfield, Wheatley Hills, 1925, John Russell Pope (a), 1917, CU, LISI, bib., previous owner J. Randolph Robinson, subsequent owner Edward F. Hutton, now part of C. W. Post College

Gould, Mrs. Edwin. Oyster Bay, 1945, CU

Guest, Frederick E. Roslyn

Handy, Parker. Glen Cove

Harriman, Henry. Jericho [Mrs. Herbert M. Harriman, LISI?]

Hepburn, F. T. Locust Valley

Hutton, Edward F. Westbury, 1942, CU; Wheatley Hills, CU, LISI, previous owner Philip Gossler

Iselin, C. Oliver. Brookville, 1917, CU

Jennings, B. B. Glen Head

Kane, John P. Locust Valley, William H. Beers (a), Louise Payson (la), LISI, bib.

*Kramer, A. Ludlow. Picket Farm, Westbury, 1920, Peabody, Wilson & Brown (a), CU, LISI, bib.

Langley, William C. Westbury, LISI

Ledyard, L. C. Jr. Syosset, 1917, Charles A. Platt (a), 1914, DC

*Lord, Franklin B. Cottsleigh, Syosset, c. 1929, William H. Beers (a), CU, LISI

*Lord, George DeForest. Overfields, Syosset, c. 1930, William H. Beers (a), CU, LISI

Maynard, Mrs. Walter E. Jericho, c. 1930, LISI

Morris, John B. Roslyn

Murray, Hugh A. Wheatley Hills

Peabody, Julian. Westbury, 1924, CU

Pratt, Herbert L. The Braes, Glen Cove, James Brite (a), 1912, James L. Greenleaf (la), CU, LISI, now Webb Institute of Naval Architecture

Preston, William P. T. Longfields, Jericho, Peabody, Wilson & Brown (a), 1913, CU

Richmond, L. M. Sunninghill, Glen Head

Roosevelt, Kermit. Oyster Bay

*Salvage, Sir Samuel Agar. Rynwood, Glen Head, 1926, Roger H. Bullard (a), 1926, AAG, CU, LISI, UO, bib., now Villa Banfi

Schmidlapp, Carl J. Mill Neck, mid-1920s, Peabody, Wilson & Brown (a), UO, bib.

Smith, R. Penn. East Williston

Smithers, F. S. Glen Cove

Stewart, Glenn. Locust Valley, CU

Taliaferro, Mrs. Eugene. Oyster Bay, CU

White, A. M. Oyster Bay

Zinsser, William. Great Neck

Long Island: Suffolk County

*Fish, Julia. Greenport, 1916, CU, LISI

Hare, Mrs. Meredith. Pigeon Hill, Huntington, Charles A. Platt (a), 1916, SPLIA

Hegeman, A. M. Southampton, c. 1917, LISI, bib.

Jackson, W. H. West Hills, 1941, CU

James, Ellery S. Southampton, Roger H. Bullard (a), 1926, bib.

Maidstone Club. East Hampton, Roger H. Bullard (a), 1922, bib.

Matheson, William J. Lloyds Neck, UO

Peabody, Julian. Huntington, 1945, CU

Peters, Henry T. Islip, CU

Plumb, Mrs. E. J. Dering Harbor, Shelter Island, 1937, CU

Poor, Charles Lane. Dering Harbor, Shelter Island

*Pruyn, Mary and Neltje. East Hampton, 1919, CU, bib.

Reed, Lansing F. Windy Hill, Lloyd Harbor, 1925, Charles A. Platt (a), 1924, CU

Ruxton, Philip. East Hampton

Swayne, Eleanor. Red House, Shinnecock Hills, Grosvenor Atterbury (a), CU

Towle, Florence M. Dering Harbor, Shelter Island. CU

Weld, Francis M. Lloyd Harbor, Charles A. Platt (a), 1911

Wood, Mrs. Willis Delano. Fort Hill House, Lloyds Neck, c. 1938, Olmsted Bros. (la), AAG

Mount Kisco

*Brewster, Mrs. Robert S. Avalon, early 1920s, Delano & Aldrich (a), 1912, CU, bib., now College of Rabbis

Cotton, Mrs. Joseph

Goodrich, David M. Charles A. Platt (a), 1912

Hammond, John Henry. Dellwood, Charles A. Platt (a), 1915, Nellie B. Allen (la), 1930s

Holter, E. O.

Lawrence, A. CU

*Magee, John. Wampus, 1916, CU, bib.

Meyer, Eugene and Agnes. Seven Springs Farm, Charles A. Platt (a), 1915, CU

Morgan, William Fellowes

Petrasch, C. S.

Preston, Lewis B.

Pruyn, Robert D. Apple Orchard, Charles A. Platt (a), 1911

Ryle, Julia. 1916, CU

Scribner, Arthur

Towne, John. Arthur Shurcliff (la), pre-1921, Fletcher Steele (a), 1921

*Tucker, Carll. Penwood, 1926, Walker & Gillette (a), 1925, Olmsted Bros. (la), 1920, CU, UO, bib.

New York City

Angell, Montgomery B. Manhattan

Arnold family plot. Woodlawn Cemetery, Brooklyn

Bell, Gordon. East 65th Street

Benkard, Henry H. Park Avenue

Clarke, J. W. Manhattan Beach, Brooklyn, UO

Cutting, Robert Fulton. UO

Erdmann, Mrs. John

Fernandez, Raoul

Forrestal, Mrs. James V. 17 Beekman Place, CU

Gordon, Mrs. Thurlow

Humbert family plot. Trinity Church, Manhattan, CU

International Garden Club. Bronx, 1931, CU

Iselin, Ernest

Kelly, Thomas Smith. 1943, CU

Lancashire, J. Henry. 11 East 69th Street

Menlesmith, Van J.

Murphy, Charles B. G.

*New York Botanical Garden. Women's Advisory Council border, Bronx, 1928, CU

Newall, Joseph. CU

Rockefeller. 1 Beekman Place, Sloan & Robertson (a), 1930

Spreckels, Geraldine. 1945, CU

Wightman, Dr. Orrin. East 65th Street, CU

Suburban New York

Allen, J. Roy. Rye, CU, UO

Angell, Montgomery B. High House, Garrison, William Platt (a), CU

Astor, Vincent. Rhinebeck

Baldwin, Mrs. Alexander. Bedford Hills, CU

Benkard, J. Philip. Tuxedo Park

Berkshire Industrial School. Canaan

Biddle, Nicholas. South Salem

Blum, Henry. Scarsdale, CU

Cahn, A. L. Hartsdale

Canfield, George T. Peekskill

Chapman, John Jay. Sylvania, Barrytown, Charles A. Platt (a), 1904

Cook, Henry A. Greenburgh

Cottier, A. E. Scarsdale

Emmet, Grenville T. Katonah, bib.

Ewing, Charles. Rye

Ewing, William. Bedford Hills

*Fahnestock, William F. Girdle Ridge, Katonah, c. 1912, Charles A. Platt (a), 1909, Olmsted Assoc. (la), 1911-12, CU, bib.

Frazier, Isobel. Garrison, CU

Hanes, Mrs. John. Millbrook

Harris, Mrs. Basil. Rye, 1942, CU

Hart, Charles. Pelham Manor

Hart, Ed. Pleasantville

Hartsonne, Douglas. Rye

Hogan, Arthur and Jefferson. Rye

Howard, Graeme. Mamaroneck, CU

*King, Frederick P. Uplands, Irvington-on-Hudson, 1933, Marian Coffin (la), 1922, CU

Lakin, Herbert. Scarsdale, CU

Matney, Margaret. Little Knoll, Brewster, 1944, CU

Melen, Mrs. N. McM. Hudson, DC

Mitchell, Ormsby. Rye, Mott B. Schmidt (a), 1920, bib.

Naumberg, George W. Groton

Osborne, Frederick. Garrison

Perkins, Thomas L. Rye, 1945, CU

Quimby, John. Brewster

Reese, Mrs. William W. New Hamburg-on-Hudson, 1936, CU

Thomas, James A. White Plains, c. 1936, CU
Tweedy, R. B. Goshen
U.S. Military Academy. Superintendent's Garden, West Point, 1936, CU
Wallerstein, Leo. Harrison
Warburg, Felix. White Plains

Upstate and Western New York State

Albright, Langdon. Buffalo, 1914, DC
Angell, Dr. Edward. Rochester
Burden, Henry. Cazenovia
Campbell, J. Hazard. East Aurora, 1931, CU
Case, Theodore W. Auburn
Clark, Mrs. C. S. Angola, CU
Clark, Stephen. Cooperstown
Clement, Stephen. East Aurora
Cooper, Dr. Henry and Katherine. Heathcote, Cooperstown
*Cooper, James Fenimore. Fynmere, Cooperstown, 1912, Charles A. Platt (la), 1911, CU, bib.
Fairchild, Charles, S. Lorenzo, Cazenovia, 1914, now Lorenzo Historic Site
Finucane, Bernard. Rochester
Forman, G. M. G. Buffalo
Gaylord, Bradley. Buffalo
Hees, J. Ledlie. Sacandaga
Houghton, Amory B. The Knoll, Corning, 1946, CU
Houghton cemetery plot. Corning
Hyde, L. F. Glens Falls
Kellogg, Spencer. Lochevan, Derby, early 1930s, CU
Knox, Seymour. Ess Kay Farm, East Aurora, 1931, CU
Mann, Stuart. Derby
Martin, Darwin D. Lakeview, 1930, CU
McGraw, F. Sears. East Aurora
Noyes, Mrs. E. H. Dansville
Petee, Harry E. Saratoga
Pratt, Francis C. Governor Yates House, Schenectady, CU, bib.
Prince, David and Winifred. Schenectady, 1942, CU
Schoelkopf, Dr. J. F. Buffalo

North Carolina (see also **Winston-Salem**)

Duke, James B. Durham
*Duke University. Sarah P. Duke Memorial Gardens, Durham, 1937, John Wister (la), 1932, CU, bib.
Eagle, Dr. Watt. Durham, CU
Gray, Bowman. Roaring Gap, 1949, CU
Hanes, Dr. Frederick. Durham, CU
Hanes, Robert. Roaring Gap, CU
Phillips, Earl N. High Point, CU
Reed, Joseph Verner
Shands, Dr. Alfred R. Durham, 1937, CU
Wade, Madison. Charlotte

Winston-Salem

Chatham, Mrs. Hugh. CU
Chatham, Mrs. Thurman. 1945, CU
Craig, Mrs. S. D. CU
Gray, Gordon. 1945, CU
Hanes, Gordon. 1946, CU
Hanes, James G. III. CU
Hanes, P. Huber. 1945, CU
Hanes, Philip
*Hanes, Ralph P. and Dewitt. 1929, CU, bib., now part of Wake Forest College
Moore, Mrs. Thomas O. CU
Mountcastle, Kenneth. CU

Ohio (see also **Chagrin Falls and Hunting Valley**)

Ashley, Meredith. Perrysburg, 1945
Bicknell, Warren. Willoughby, Olmsted Bros. (la), 1916, CU
Bonnerwitz, Lee R. Van Wert
Burns, James A. Columbus, CU
Burton, Courtney. Gates Mills
Burton, R. C. Lanesville
Chatfield, William Hayden. Hunt's End, Madeira, c. 1928
*Clapp, Willard M. Cleveland Heights, 1926, Meade & Hamilton (a), 1926, Warren Manning (la), 1922, CU, bib.
Corning, Mrs. Henry. Bratenahl, CU
Dodge, Henry M. Perrysburg, 1945, CU
Garfield, James R. Lawnfield, West Mentor,

now James A. Garfield National Historic Site

Halstead, Mrs. John. Perrysburg, CU

Hanna, Mrs. Howard. Kirtland, CU

Hoffman, Clare J. Washington Township, 1945, CU

Humphrey, George M. Holiday Hill Farm, Mentor, 1946, CU

Huntington, F. R. Columbus, c. 1927, CU

Ireland, Mrs. James D. Bratenahl

MacNichol, George P. Perrysburg, 1944, CU

*Mather, William Gwinn and Elizabeth. Gwinn, Bratenahl, 1914, Charles A. Platt (a), 1907, Warren Manning (la), 1906, bib.

Meade, George H. Dayton, bib.

Newell, John. Mentor

Ormond, M. G. Perrysburg, CU

Parmelee, Mrs. James. Parmelee Farm, Painesville, 1915, CU

Perkins, Jacob B. Mentor

Robinson, Jefferson. Toledo, CU

Secor, George Barnes. Perrysburg, 1944, CU

*Seiberling, Frank A. and Gertrude. Stan Hywet Hall, Akron, 1928, Charles S. Schneider (a), Warren Manning (la), 1911, bib., open to the public

Stranahan, Duane. Perrysburg, 1945, CU

Stranahan, Frank. Toledo, CU

Stranahan, Robert A. Ottowa Hills, Toledo, 1936, CU

Sullivan, Mrs. Corliss. Gates Mills, Warren Manning (la), CU

Vail, Herman L. Bratenahl

White, Thomas. Cleveland, CU

Wilbur, Rollin A. Cleveland, CU, DC

Chagrin Falls and Hunting Valley

Bishop, Dr. Robert H. Warren Manning (la), 1916, CU

Burke, E. S. Jr. 1931, Meade & Hamilton (a), Warren Manning (la), CU, bib.

Herrick, Parmely. DC

Hunting Valley Town Hall. CU

Ingalls, David S. 1937, Carl Rowley (a), CU

Mather, Amasa S. Warren Manning (la), 1916

White, Holden. CU

White, Thomas

*White, Windsor T. Halfred Farms, 1919, Bryant Fleming (a), Warren Manning (la), 1919, CU, bib.

Wick, Myron A. Warren Manning (la)

Pennsylvania (see also **Philadelphia area**)

Belin, D'Andelot. Waverly

Brock, Henry G. Muncy

Case, Theodore W. White Mills, CU

Curry, Mrs. Henry M. Sewickley, 1945, CU

Goodyear, C. W. Lewistown

Hanks, George J. Bradford

Heinz, Howard. Pittsburgh

Ingersoll, Frank. Pittsburgh, 1937, CU

Lucas, Maitland B. Bucks County, 1941, CU

McClintic, H. H. Pittsburgh

Milligan, Robert F. Sewickley

Pinchot, Gifford. Grey Towers, Milford

Richards, Mrs. Ralph S. Sewickley, 1947, CU

Riley, Edward. Lumberville, 1939, CU

Robertson, N. G. Waverly, CU

Scranton, W. W. Scranton

Smith, William Watson. Ligonier, 1937, CU; Pittsburgh, CU

Suydam, Fred D. White Mills, 1941, CU

Thomson, Frank. Devon

Van Voorhes, H. W. Sewickley

Warren, Edward. Waverly, CU

Philadelphia area

Andrews, Schofield. Philadelphia

Banklie, Archibald. Wayne

Biddle, Craig. Wayne

Foerderer, Mrs. Percival. Bryn Mawr, CU

Gibson, Mary K. Philadelphia, CU

Gilpin, John C. Chestnut Hill

Liversidge, T. K. Narbeth, 1943, CU

Lloyd, Horatio. Haverford

Mills, Paul. Saint Davids

Morgan, Randal and Frances. Wyndmoor, Chestnut Hill, Olmsted Bros. (la), 1897, Marian Coffin (la), 1934, Fletcher Steele (la), 1935

Morris, I. Wistar. Chestnut Hill, UO

*Morris, Samuel. Edgehill, Chestnut Hill, 1922, CU, bib.

Paul, A. J. Drexel. Box Hill, Radnor, Charles A. Platt (a), 1914, CU

Rivinis, E. F. Chestnut Hill

Smith, W. Hinckle. Timberline, Bryn Mawr, Charles A. Platt (a), 1907, Olmsted Bros. (la), 1907

*Starr, Isaac Tatnall. Laverock Hill, Chestnut Hill, 1915, Charles A. Platt (a), 1915, AAG, CU, bib.

Steel, A. G. B. Chestnut Hill

Strubing, Philip. Chestnut Hill, c. 1940, Warren Manning (la), 1917

Thomson, Anne. Bryn Mawr

Tyler, George. Elkins Park

Warden, William Gray. Philadelphia

Rhode Island

Allen, Mrs. Frederick H. The Mount, Newport, 1932, CU

Lihme, C. Bai. Watch Hill

Thacher, T. D. Watch Hill

South Carolina

Keane, Jerome. Aiken

Kenefick, T. S. Aiken, CU

Knox, Seymour. Aiken, 1930

Legendre, Sidney. Berkeley County

William, Clark. Camden, 1925, CU

Tennessee

Ewing, Mrs. Henry O. Lookout Mountain, CU

Martin, C. G. Chattanooga, CU

Patten, Mrs. George. Riverview, CU

Texas

Brown, Lutcher. Oak Court, San Antonio, CU, bib.

Dickson, Mrs. J. F. Houston, CU

Farish, Stephen. Ravenna, Houston, John F. Staub (a), 1934, CU, bib.

Green, John. Houston, CU

Hogg, Ima. Bayou Bend, Houston, 1920s, John F. Staub (a), 1926, bib.

Neff, Mrs. Richard. Houston, CU, bib.

Paddock, W. A. Houston, 1936, CU

Sharp, Mrs. W. B. Houston, CU

Stewart, Graham. Graham, c. 1934, CU

Weiss, Mrs. Harry C. Houston, John F. Staub (a), 1930, CU

Winston, James O. Jr. Houston, 1939, John F. Staub (a), 1938, CU

Wrightsman, Mrs. Stafford. Houston, CU

Vermont

Bennington Library. Bennington

Billings, Frederick, Julia, and Elizabeth. Woodstock, 1912, Charles A. Platt (la), 1899, Martha Brookes Hutcheson (la), 1902, CU, now Marsh-Billings National Historical Park

Brooks, Henry. Woodstock

Brown, Horace. North Mowing, Springfield, 1914, CU

Brown, J. Russell. Malletts Bay

Burgess, Mrs. F. V. Burlington, CU

Davis, Gilbert. Windsor

Field, William. Rutland, 1947, CU

*Jennings, Philip B. Bennington, 1914, Albro & Lindeberg (a), 1912, CU, bib.

Johnson, Guy B. Bennington, DC

Judd, Mrs. Edith. Redding

Matney, Margaret. Sheddsville

McCullough, J. G. North Bennington

Mead, Taylor. Windsor, 1943, CU

Parmelee, Robert M. Old Bennington, 1926, CU

Proctor, Redfield. Proctor, 1935, CU

Shoemaker, Mrs. M. M. Old Bennington, CU

Squiers, Charles B. Bennington

Webb, Captain Watson. Shelburne

Willson, Mrs. E. V. K. Rutland, 1931, CU

Woodstock Congregational Church. Woodstock

Woodstock Railway Station. Woodstock

Virginia

Davis, T. B. Middleburg, 1933, CU

*Devore, Col. Daniel B. Chatham Manor, Fredericksburg, 1924, AAG, CU, bib., subsequent owner John Lee Pratt, now part of Fredericksburg and Spotsylvania Battlefields Memorial National Military Park, open to the public

Gildersleeve, Mrs. Alfred. Charlottesville, 1940, CU

Greenhalgh, George P. Springsbury, Berryville, 1945, CU

Jackson, Mrs. Cary. Keswick; Orange, 1942, CU

Jenkins, Edward. Millwood, 1936, CU

Lloyd, Mrs. Stacy. Millwood, CU

Pratt, John Lee. Chatham Manor, Fredericksburg, 1931. See *Devore (above)

Reed, William. Sabot, 1937, CU

Ruddock, A. B. Richmond

Warburg, [Frederick]. Middleburg, CU

Washington

Merrill, Richard D. Seattle, 1915, Charles A. Platt (a), 1909, Lord & Schryver (la), 1929, Thomas D. Church (la), 1960s, CU, UO, bib.

Washington, D.C.

Corbin, Henry

Grayson, Cary T. UO

Murdock, J. E. CU

*Parmelee, James. The Causeway, 1914, Charles A. Platt (a), 1912, CU, bib.

Poor, E. B.

Stewart, Alexander

Szechenyi, Count Laszlo. UO

Townsend, Richard

Walcott, F. C.

West Virginia

Goldthorpe, Mrs. Edward C. Charleston, CU

Ketcham, Mrs. D. A. Charleston, CU

Wisconsin

Ingram, Erskine B. Eau Claire, Charles A. Platt (a), 1921

Other locations

Dubuc, J. E. Chicoutimi, Quebec

Truesdale, M. D. Bermuda

Unknown locations

Black, Durel. CU

Booker, N. J.

Cabot

Clark, Emory

Coolidge, T. Jefferson

Craig, William

Elsas

Ferguson

Hackett, J. K.

Hanson. CU

Harvey

Hayes

Hill, G. W.

Hill, Francis Powell. CU

Hopkins, D. Luke

Jander

La Montagne. CU

Laughlin, George Jr.

Lawrence

Loening

Malone, Halsey

Mellen, R. B.

Miller, George

Miller, Rachel

Newman

Nugent

O'Brien

Penn

Poor, Garnet

Reilly

Sanders Memorial

Schoelkopf, Alfred

Schoelkopf, W.

Sigma Gamma

Straus, Mrs. H. H. CU

Strauss, Percy

Upton

Warren, Cornelia W.

Watts

Whitehouse, Mrs. Norman

Willard, Mrs. Joseph

NOTES

INTRODUCTION
A History of Women in Landscape Architecture

1. Elvenia Slossom, *Pioneer American Gardening* (New York: Coward-McCann, 1951), 241, 217.

2. Alice Morse Earle, *Old Time Gardens* (New York: Macmillan, 1901), 2.

3. For a discussion of the gendered division of labor on the farm, see William Ross, *Landscaping the Farmstead*, U.S. Office of Education, Vocational Education Bulletin no. 189, 1938.

4. U. P. Hedrick, *A History of Horticulture in America to 1860*, With an Addendum of Books Published from 1861 to 1920 by Elisabeth Woodburn (Portland: Timber Press, 1988). See also Beverly Seaton, "American Sources for the Study of American Gardens, 1890–1930," symposium paper presented at H. F. du Pont Winterthur Museum and Garden, Winterthur, Del., 10 March 1979; and Seaton, "The Garden Autobiography," *Garden History, Journal of the Garden History Society* 7 (Spring 1979).

5. Louisa Johnson, *Every Woman Her Own Flower Gardener*, 1871.

6. Harriet Beecher Stowe, *Household Papers and Stories* (Boston: Houghton Mifflin, 1864).

7. See Alison Knight, "An Examination of the History of the Lowthorpe School of Landscape Architecture for Women, Groton, Mass., 1901–1945" (Master's thesis, Cornell University, 1986). Despite their advocacy of women in the profession, the founders of Lowthorpe envisioned a special role for women as horticultural assistants in nurseries, estates, and landscape architecture offices, as teachers of gardening, and as gardening consultants. The modesty of these goals scarcely reflects the school's track record: between 1901 and 1945, Lowthorpe produced almost three hundred accomplished landscape architects.

8. Dorothy May Anderson, *Women, Design, and the Cambridge School* (Mesa, Ariz.: PDA Publishers, 1980). The first curriculum of the school included design, construction, office practice, drawing, horticulture, and history. Frost, seeking to improve the opportunities for his graduates to get commissions, added the word "Domestic" to the name of the school in 1920. He eventually removed it, realizing that the addition encouraged a perception that women were especially or even exclusively qualified for residential design. Anderson's history of the Cambridge School is an invaluable resource for historians of women in landscape architecture.

9. Ruth Wanger, *What Girls Can Do* (New York: Henry Holt, 1926).

10. E. W. Weaver, *Profitable Vocations for Girls* (Chicago: Laidlaw Brothers, 1924), 103–4.

11. Olmsted quoted in Anderson, *Women, Design, and the Cambridge School*, 20.

12. These views were expressed by men in the American Society of Landscape Architects as recently as 1973 in response to a questionnaire regarding attitudes toward women in practice.

13. Leslie Rose Close, *Portrait of an Era in Landscape Architecture: The Photographs of Mattie Edwards Hewitt*, exh. cat. (Bronx, N.Y.: Wave Hill, 1983).

14. Henry Frost quoted in Anderson, *Women, Design, and the Cambridge School*, 19.

15. Marjorie Sewell Cautley was one of the few women with a thriving career in estate design who made the transition to community planning. Her major work was Sunnyside Gardens, with Henry Wright and Clarence Stein. Another landscape architect who adapted to the changes in the profession was Helen Bullard, who worked in the offices of both Warren Manning and Annette Hoyt Flanders. Bullard worked on the bath houses at Jones Beach and on the Southern State Parkway, the Grand Central Parkway, and the Montauk Highway, all in New York. In 1938, an article in the *New York Times* featured her with eight other—male—landscape architects who had been hired to design the 1939 New York World's Fair.

CHAPTER ONE
Early Years

1. "House and Garden's Own Hall of Fame," *House and Garden,* June 1933, 50; "Mrs. Ellen Shipman, Landscape Designer," obituary, *New York Times,* 29 March 1950, 29. The term "good taste" has a variety of sources, including Mariana van Rensselaer's *Art Out-of-Doors, Hints on Good Taste in Gardening* (1893) and Elsie de Wolfe's *The House in Good Taste* (1913).

2. Working steadily for thirty-five years (1912–47) at the average rate of fifteen to twenty projects per year, Shipman would have completed approximately six hundred. It is likely that the final number was higher.

3. Shipman quoted in Anne Petersen, "Women Take the Lead in Landscape Art," *New York Times,* 13 March 1938.

4. Preface, Garden Note Book (partial contents in box 10, folder 15, Cornell; hereafter cited as GNB), 1.

5. Shipman quoted in Peterson, "Women Take the Lead."

6. Foreword, GNB, 3.

7. The date of Shipman's birth is cited in a letter of 27 June 1944 from her to her executors (Nancy Streeter, private collection). The location of her birth is based on information from Streeter and other sources.

8. Ellen McGowan Biddle, *Reminiscences of a Soldier's Wife* (Philadelphia: J. B. Lippincott, 1907), 154.

9. Foreword, GNB, 2.

10. Biddle, *Reminiscences,* 136.

11. Ibid., 188–89.

12. Ellen McGowan Biddle, *Recollections* (Boston: Small, Maynard, 1920), 3; foreword, GNB, 11–12.

13. Foreword, GNB, 3.

14. Biddle, *Reminiscences,* 220.

15. Deborah E. Van Buren, "Landscape Architecture and Gardens in the Cornish Colony: The Careers of Rose Nichols, Ellen Shipman, and Frances Duncan," *Women's Studies* 14 (September 1988): 367–88; Frances McCormic, interview with Van Buren, 13 August 1985.

16. The Harvard Annex, located on Appian Way, Cambridge, was established in 1879 "to provide women with access to a Harvard education." During Shipman's term the school was the Society for the Collegiate Instruction of Women.

17. Nicholas B. Angell, interview with author, 19 January 1994; Angell, interview with Deborah E. Van Buren, August 1985, in "Women and Landscape Architecture: Rose Nichols and Ellen Shipman in the Cornish Colony," paper presented at the annual meeting of the American Studies Association, San Diego, 1985, n. 48.

18. Mary Lucy Wilkins Rogers, undated typescript (Annie Ware Winsor Allen Papers, Radcliffe College Archives, Schlesinger Library, Radcliffe College, Cambridge, Mass.).

19. *National Cyclopaedia of American Biography* (New York: James T. White, 1962), 45:396–97.

20. Harvard University Directory (1910) lists Louis Shipman as c. 1892–93, but the trail ends in *Special Students* (1894–95) grade reports, which note his withdrawal on 12 April 1893, two months after his roommate Herbert Croly temporarily withdrew from classes.

21. Angell-author interview; also Angell–Van Buren interview, n. 11.

CHAPTER TWO
Life in the Cornish Colony

1. The date of this trip is uncertain; an early draft of the Garden Note Book, written fifty years after the event, states that Shipman's first visit was August 1894, but subsequent versions state 1895.

2. For an excellent overview of the social life of the Cornish Colony, see Deborah Kay Meador, "The Making of a Landscape Architect: Ellen Biddle Shipman and Her Years at the Cornish Art Colony" (M.L.A. thesis, Cornell University, 1989), 40–46.

3. Foreword, GNB, 1.

4. The script was written by Louis Shipman and Percy MacKaye, with music by the composer Arthur Whiting performed by the Boston Symphony Orchestra. John H. Dryfhout et al., *A Circle of Friends: Art Colonies of Cornish and Dublin* (Durham, N.H.: University Art Galleries, 1985), 52, 110.

5. Frances Grimes, "Reminiscences," undated typescript (Dartmouth College Library, Hanover, N.H.), 1; *New York Daily Tribune*, 11 August 1907, quoted in Dryfhout et al., *Circle of Friends*, 40.

6. Virginia Colby, private collection, Cornish, N.H. See "Ellen Biddle Shipman—Landscape Architect: 1869–1950," *Windsor (Vt.) Chronicle*, 23 January 1987. In a letter she wrote to Lawrence W. Rittenoure, 15 June 1944 (Cornell), Shipman states that Poins House was theirs for ten years; they leased it using the money from Louis's story "The Curious Courtship of Kate Poins." However, the Shipmans' ten-year lease of the house began in 1895, six years before the publication of Louis's story.

7. Grimes, "Reminiscences," 1.

8. One of the only published views of this garden is in Frances Duncan, "The Gardens of Cornish," *Century Magazine*, May 1906, 8.

9. Mary Caroline Crawford, "Homes and Gardens of Cornish," *House Beautiful*, April 1906, 12–14.

10. Foreword, GNB, 2; design chapter, GNB, 35–36.

11. Rose Standish Nichols, "A Hilltop Garden in New Hampshire," *House Beautiful*, March 1924, 237; Duncan, "Gardens of Cornish," 18. For further information on Duncan, who was a summer resident of Cornish and a prolific writer, see Virginia Lopez Begg, "Frances Duncan: The 'New Woman' in the Garden," *Journal of the New England Garden History Society* 2 (1992): 29–35.

12. Foreword, GNB, 2.

13. Alan Crawford, "New Life for an Artists' Village," *Country Life*, 24 January 1980, 252–54.

14. See Judith B. Tankard, "William Robinson and the Art of the Book," *Hortus* 27 (Autumn 1993): 21–30.

15. Helena Rutherford Ely, *A Woman's Hardy Garden* (New York: Macmillan, 1903), and Alice Morse Earle, *Old Time Gardens* (New York: Macmillan, 1902). See Beverly Seaton, "Gar-

dening Books for the Commuter's Wife, 1900–1937," *Landscape* 28 (1985): 41–47. See also Virginia Tuttle Clayton, "Reminiscence and Revival: The Old-Fashioned Garden, 1890–1910," *Magazine Antiques*, April 1990, 892–905; May Brawley Hill, "Grandmother's Garden," *Magazine Antiques*, November 1992, 726–35.

16. David W. Levy, *Herbert Croly of "The New Republic"* (Princeton, N.J.: Princeton University Press, 1985), 77–79. The Crolys are buried next to Shipman in the Gilkey Cemetery, adjacent to Brook Place, in Plainfield, N.H.

17. See John H. Dryfhout, "The Gardens of Augustus Saint-Gaudens," *House and Garden*, December 1985, 144–48, 199; Marion Pressley and Cynthia Zaitzevsky, *Cultural Landscape Report for Saint-Gaudens National Historic Site* (Boston: National Park Service, 1993).

18. Mary Wilkinson Mount, "The Gardens of Cornish," *Suburban Life*, March 1914, 133. For further information on Parrish's garden diaries and an excellent study of the making of the garden at Northcote, see William Noble, "Northcote: An Artist's New Hampshire Garden," *Journal of the New England Garden History Society* 2 (1992): 1–9

19. Dryfhout et al., *Circle of Friends*, 50; Grimes, "Reminiscences," 1; Meador, "Making of a Landscape Architect," 45.

20. Louis wrote for several publications, including *Leslie's Weekly* during 1895–96, and occasionally collaborated with fellow Cornishites, including Churchill and Remington, rewriting their works for the stage. His first published book, *Urban Dialogues* (1896), is a witty spoof on urban life, but his romantic comedy *D'Arcy of the Guards* gave his reputation a needed boost; it was dedicated to Shipman's brother Nicholas Biddle.

21. Margaret Homer Nichols Shurcliff, *Lively Days* (Taipei: Literature House, 1965), 35, as quoted in Virginia Colby, "Plainfield and the Cornish Colony through Biographies," in *Choice White Pines and Good Land: A History of Plainfield and Meriden, New Hampshire,* ed. Nancy Norwalk and Harold Zea (Portsmouth, N.H.: Peter E. Randall, 1991), 366; Harry B. Fuller, letter to Shipman, 29 August 1906 (Dartmouth).

22. Foreword, GNB, 3.

23. Property agreement (box 8, folder 12, Cornell) refers to John Gilkey's deeds to Ellen Biddle Shipman dated 18 April 1903 (Sullivan County Record of Deeds, vol. 156, 309) and 16 October 1906 (vol. 166, 196). Plainfield tax records indicate that the Shipmans were first taxed for 182 acres on the Gilkey farm in 1904 (Plainfield Historical Society). They probably moved to Brook Place in 1906 after their ten-year lease on Poins House was up. Hugh Mason Wade, in *A Brief History of Cornish, 1763–1974* (Hanover, N.H.: University Press of New England, 1976), states that the Shipmans acquired the farm in 1902 (69–70); John H. Dryfhout (letter to Catherine Zusy, 24 September 1984) maintains that the Shipmans lived at Poins House from 1897 until 1907, rather than from 1895 to 1905; foreword, GNB, 4.

24. The addition is dated 1911 (William Macdonald, McLaughry Associates, Realtors, West Lebanon, N.H.). Platt's biographer, Keith Morgan, doubts that Platt had anything to do with its design (telephone interview with author, 7 July 1994).

25. Design chapter, GNB, 1.

26. G. H. Edgell, *The American Architecture of To-Day* (New York: Charles Scribner's Sons, 1928), 125.

27. Hewitt's photographs were published in "A New Hampshire House and Garden," *House and Garden*, March 1924, 75–77.

28. Foreword, GNB, 4.

29. These articles include Herbert C. Wise, "A Day at Northcote, A House and Garden in New Hampshire," *House and Garden*, June 1902, 244, 249; Crawford, "Homes and Gardens of Cor-

nish"; Duncan, "Gardens of Cornish"; Duncan, "An Artist's New Hampshire Garden," *Country Life in America*, March 1907, 516–20, 554–58; "A Cornish House and Garden," *Architectural Record*, October 1907, 288–98; Duncan, "A Cornish Garden," *Country Life in America*, March 1908, 507–8; Mount, "Gardens of Cornish," 133–36, 184; Rose Standish Nichols, "A Hilltop Garden in New Hampshire," *House Beautiful*, March 1924, 237–39, 290. Quotation from Crawford, "Homes and Gardens," 12–14.

30. Nichols, "Hilltop Garden," 237. Platt's *Italian Gardens* was published in a new edition, with additional plates and an overview by Keith N. Morgan, by Sagapress/Timber Press (New York) in 1993.

31. Royal Cortissoz, introduction, *Monograph on the Work of Charles A. Platt* (New York: Architectural Book Publishing, 1913), v–vi.

32. Lazarus sold High Court in 1900 to Norman Hapgood, editor of *Collier's Weekly* (a magazine to which Louis Shipman contributed), who in turn sold it to A. Conger Goodyear in 1912. Shipman designed a planting plan, dated September 1914, for Mrs. Goodyear. James Farley, letter to Deborah Van Buren, 20 August 1985.

33. Wilhelm Miller, "An 'Italian Garden' That Is Full of Flowers," *Country Life in America*, March 1905, 485.

34. Richard G. Kenworthy, "Bringing the World to Brookline: The Gardens of Larz and Isabel Anderson," *Journal of Garden History* 11 (1991): 228; E.T., "The Garden of 'Weld,'" *House and Garden*, March 1904, 106.

35. George Taloumis, "Rose Standish Nichols," *Boston Sunday Globe,* 16 September 1956. After taking design lessons from Platt around 1889, Nichols apprenticed with the New York architect Thomas Hastings and then studied at the Ecole de Beaux Arts in Paris and with H. Inigo Triggs, the author of *Formal Gardens in England and Scotland* (1902). For more information on Nichols, see Van Buren, "Landscape Architecture and Gardens in the Cornish Colony," 368–88.

36. "Going to School," in Norwalk and Zea, *Choice White Pines*, 289; Shipman, "How I Teach My Own Children," *Ladies Home Journal*, September 1911, 60.

37. Candace Wheeler, "Home Weaving in Country Homes," *Country Life in America*, July 1903, 198–200; see also Beatrice Clark, "Mothers' and Daughters' Club and Mothers' and Daughters' Rug Industry, "in Norwalk and Zea, *Choice White Pines*, 201–9.

38. Shipman, letter to Gertrude Eisendrath Kuh, c. 1942, quoted in Mary Elizabeth Fitzsimons, "Outdoor Architecture for the Midwest: The Modern Residential Landscapes of Gertrude Eisendrath Kuh, 1935–1977" (M.L.A. thesis, University of Minnesota, January 1994), 18.

39. Nancy Streeter, interview with author, 2 September 1994. Amy Cogswell, who became director of the Lowthorpe School in Groton, Mass., in 1916, may have worked briefly as a tutor and nanny for the Shipman children during a summer break while she was a student at Lowthorpe. Frances McCormic, interview with Deborah E. Van Buren, 2 August 1985, transcript, 6.

CHAPTER THREE
Collaboration with Charles Platt

1. Foreword, GNB, 4.

2. Shipman's correspondence with the Moravian Pottery and Tile Works regarding her work at Fynmere, generally regarded as her earliest work, dates between 17 March and 22 July 1913. See Catherine Zusy, "A Unity of Design in the American Spirit: James Fenimore Cooper II's 'Fynmere,'" paper written for Cooperstown History Museum Studies Program, 1984.

3. Shipman, letter to Mrs. Roy Chapin, Detroit, Mich., 25 May 1946 (box 9, folder 5, Cornell).

4. See Judith B. Tankard, "The Influence of British Garden Literature on American Garden Design during the Country Place Era," in *Proceedings, Masters of American Garden Design III,* ed. Robin Karson (New York: Garden Conservancy, 1995).

5. Keith N. Morgan, *Charles A. Platt: The Artist as Architect* (Cambridge/New York: MIT/Architectural History Foundation, 1985), 251. Two articles confirm Shipman's role as the garden designer. There are five letters about the job; all are on Shipman's Cornish letterhead.

6. Shipman, "Design and Construction," transcript of lecture given for the St. Paul (Minn.) Garden Club, 5 February 1935, 27, 30 (Streeter collection).

7. Henry S. F. Cooper, letter to Keith Morgan, 6 January 1977.

8. Shipman was not identified by name in "Looking over the Garden Wall," *Country Life in America,* March 1917, 68–69, but was in *House and Garden's Book of Gardens* (New York: Condé Nast, 1921), 81.

9. Plans date from May 1914 to 1919. Six photographs of the project were shown in the Architectural League of New York annual exhibition in 1924.

10. Shipman did not return to Gwinn until the early 1930s, when she consulted with Mather's wife, Elizabeth Ring Mather. See Robin Karson, *The Muses of Gwinn: Art and Nature in a Garden Designed by Warren H. Manning, Charles A. Platt, and Ellen Biddle Shipman* (New York: Sagapress/Library of American Landscape History, 1995), 135–37; Karson, "Gwinn: A Collaborative Design by Charles A. Platt and Warren H. Manning," *Journal of the New England Garden History Society* 3 (1993): 29.

11. Morgan, *Charles A. Platt,* 248. See illustrations of Platt's garden in *Monograph on the Work of Charles A. Platt* (1913) and additional illustrations in "Four Views of the Garden at the Estate of William Fahnestock, Esq., Katonah, New York," *Journal of the International Garden Club* 2 (September 1918): 360–64.

12. In 1929, Shipman handed over responsibility for the garden to the new Oregon firm of Elizabeth Lord and Edith Schryver; Schryver had been her employee in New York.

13. Design chapter, GNB, 18.

14. Samuel Howe, *American Country Houses of To-Day* (New York: Architectural Book Publishing, 1915), 6.

15. After Marion Alger gave the property to the Detroit Institute of Arts, Shipman redesigned one of the areas as a knot garden in 1936.

16. Design chapter, GNB, 38.

17. In his project list for Platt, Keith Morgan cites jobs for the following clients as showing evidence of Shipman's involvement: Russell Alger, James F. Cooper, William Fahnestock, James Parmelee, A. J. Drexel Paul, the Misses Pruyn, William Speed, Isaac Starr, Henry Stephens, and Clark Williams (*Charles A. Platt,* 239–62).

18. Shipman, letter to Ernest Kanzler, Detroit, Mich., 3 June 1946 (box 9, folder 9, Cornell); Edith Stern, interview with Pamela Bardo, 3 July 1977, typescript (Longue Vue), 2. Shipman later claimed that she never designed plantings unless she did the entire design. Letter to Mrs. Roy D. Chapin, Detroit, Mich., 25 May 1946 (box 9, folder 5, Cornell).

CHAPTER FOUR
A Style of Her Own

1. Design chapter, GNB, 1; "Mrs. Ellen Shipman, Famous Landscape Architect, Thrills Hearers," *Winston-Salem Journal,* 8 October 1932.

2. Design chapter, GNB, 6.

3. Shipman, letter to Mrs. Roy Chapin, Detroit, Mich., 17 June 1946 (box 9, folder 5, Cornell); Shipman, letter to Mrs. Willis G. Wilmot, Hermitage, Tenn., 28 June 1945 (box 8, folder 35, Cornell).

4. Karson, *Muses of Gwinn*, 81, 83.

5. Shipman quoted in Helen Grant Wilson, "Good Counsel for Gardeners: Hosta or Funkia Stages Comeback in Gardens," *Cleveland Plain Dealer,* 7 May 1942.

6. Preface no. 1, GNB, 2.

7. Design chapter, GNB, 2, 7.

8. Shipman's notation appears on the reverse of the plan: "The first plan I ever made for a garden—Dora Murdocks, Baltimore" (Streeter collection).

9. Other Lindeberg clients for whom Shipman is known to have done garden plans are Eugene du Pont, Greenville, Del., 1917; Mrs. Frederick G. Achelis, Greenwich, Conn., 1919; and R. T. Vanderbilt, Greens Farms, Conn., 1939. She may also have carried out commissions for Laurance Armour, Lake Forest, Ill., and William L. Hanley Jr., Greenwich, Conn.

10. Elizabeth Leonard Strang, a 1910 graduate of Cornell College of Agriculture, remained with Shipman for only about a year before she moved to Leominster, Mass., when she began teaching at the Lowthorpe School (where Shipman would also maintain close professional ties). Strang's formal training would eventually far exceed Shipman's—she later apprenticed with three influential practitioners: Ferrucio Vitale, Carl Pilat, and John Nolan. See Daniel W. Krall, "Ellen Biddle Shipman: Dean of Women Landscape Architects," undated manuscript, 113, and Krall, "Elizabeth Leonard Strang: Teacher and Advocate for Landscape Architecture," undated manuscript (both, Department of Landscape Architecture, Cornell University).

11. Lucinda Brockway, interview with author, 24 August 1994.

12. Two articles that chronicle the inclusion of the garden in the 1923 Architectural League of New York annual exhibition give varying credit: the caption to an illustration that appears in both gives credit to Shipman in one (*Garden Magazine,* June 1924, 279) and to Greenleaf in the other (*House and Garden,* June 1924, 54).

13. Design chapter, GNB, 38.

14. Shipman quoted in Lamar Sparks, "A Landscape Architect Discusses Gardens," *Better Homes and Gardens,* November 1930, 20.

15. "A House in New Canaan, Connecticut," *House Beautiful,* January 1924, 41; on the Gossler garden, see also *Garden Magazine and Home Builder,* October 1924, 91.

16. No plan for the garden has been found, but drawings for the pergola and other ornamental details survive. Shipman's pencil sketch of the fountain terrace is dated March 1916.

17. Jekyll's book was first published in 1908 as *Colour in the Flower Garden* (London: Country Life). Shipman owned the third edition, published in 1914.

18. Fletcher Steele, ed., *House Beautiful Gardening Manual* (Boston: Atlantic Monthly, 1926), 10.

CHAPTER FIVE
The New York Office

1. Mary Shipman briefly attended Ethel Walker's School but harbored more interest in horses and riding than books. Evan, Ellen's son, had left the Groton School in 1917 at age thirteen after a poor academic performance and entered the Salisbury School in July 1919, which he left without explanation in 1922. Hoping that Evan would attend Harvard, the Shipmans sent him to Europe for tutoring, but he soon drifted into the Paris-based "lost generation." Mary and Evan's older sister, Ellen, who attended St. Timothy's in Maryland, was married in 1918. Streeter-author interview;

Herbert Channick, memoir on Evan Shipman, privately published on the occasion of the 50th reunion of Evan's class at Groton School.

2. Robert A. M. Stern, Gregory Gilmartin, and Thomas Mellins, *New York 1930: Architecture and Urbanism between Two World Wars* (New York: Rizzoli, 1987), 433 n. 324; Shipman, letter to John N. Wheeler, New York City, 15 June 1945 (box 8, folder 38, Cornell).

3. "A House on Beekman Place, New York," *House Beautiful*, November 1927, 513–16, 568–69.

4. Among women who had landscape businesses in New York City in the early 1920s were Nellie B. Allen; Ruth Bramley Dean; Agnes Selkirk Clark, who briefly worked for Shipman before opening her own office in 1922; Marian Cruger Coffin, who worked in the city from 1910 until 1927; Beatrix Jones Farrand, who came in 1900; Annette Hoyt Flanders, who worked there sporadically from 1914 to 1942; Martha Brookes Hutcheson; Mary Deputy Lamson; Louise Payson; and Isabella Pendleton.

5. Shipman quoted in "Professional Opinions," *Lowthorpe School Catalogue,* 1926–27, Groton, Mass. Curiously, one source lists Shipman's name among the alumnae. See Richard A. Schneider, "Lowthorpe" (thesis, Rhode Island School of Design, 1988), 86.

6. Shipman quoted in *Lowthorpe School Catalogue,* 1925, 4.

7. Frances McCormic, telephone interview with Daniel Krall, 10 January 1990.

8. Elizabeth Lord and Edith Schryver's Salem office was the first on the West coast to be run entirely by women. Among their office archives at the University of Oregon are documents from two dozen projects that Schryver worked on while in Shipman's office. Kenneth Helphand, "Lord and Schryver," in *Pioneers of American Landscape Design*, ed. Charles Birnbaum and Lisa Crowder (Washington, D.C.: National Park Service/Preservation Assistance Division, 1993), 80–82.

Louise Payson and Eleanor Christie roomed together while working in the Cornish office during their summer breaks from Lowthorpe. Upon graduation, Christie returned to Ohio and opened her own office in Cincinnati in 1928. Noel Dorsey Vernon, letter to author, June 1994.

Less well-known employees were Louise Jocelyn, Carol Farley, Irmgard Berger Graham, Virginia Prince, Eleanor Roche, Mary Louise Speed, and Florence Stroh. Draftsmen were Louanne Eggleston, Shirley Harris, Helen Kippax, Louise Leland, Katherine Rogers, and Doris Turnball. These names have been culled from Shipman's office correspondence, notations in her notebooks, news articles, and references by Knight, Krall, Meador, McCormic, and Van Buren.

9. McCormic-Krall interview; Frances McCormic went to Oberlin College for several years and, subsequently, to the University of Wisconsin, where she heard about the Lowthorpe School. McCormic–Van Buren interview.

10. Shipman, letter to Mrs. Willis G. Wilmot, Hermitage, Tenn., 28 June 1945 (box 8, folder 35, Cornell).

11. McCormic, memo to Daniel Krall, August 1989 (Streeter collection); Eleanor Christie, interview with Noel Dorsey Vernon, 29 July 1985, transcript, 2.

12. Shipman, invoice to Mrs. Douglas Conoley, Cumberstone, Md., 15 May 1946 (box 9, folder 5, Cornell).

13. Irene Seiberling Harrison, interview with Robin Karson, Stan Hywet Hall, Akron, Ohio, 18 February 1991.

14. Nancy Streeter, interview with author, 21 June 1994.

15. Anne Bruce Haldeman, introduction, GNB.

16. Shipman, letter to Mrs. Carll Tucker, Mt. Kisco, N.Y., 14 June 1946 (box 9, folder 1, Cornell).

17. Shipman, letter to Mr. and Mrs. William G. Mather, Cleveland, Ohio, 15 November 1945 (box 8, folder 54, Cornell).

18. Viscountess Wolseley, *In a College Garden* (London: John Murray, 1916), 104.

19. Shipman will, 9 November 1948, Probate Records, Newport, N.H. According to the terms, Meyette was to receive a lump sum of $1,500 plus $3,800 for 38 years of service, a substantial remembrance.

20. Streeter-author interview, 21 June 1994.

21. Clark, "Mothers' and Daughters' Club," 208 and ill. 333. The Plainfield Historical Society has a collection of hand-colored glass slides of these gardens.

22. Matthew Josephson, "Evan Shipman: Poet and Horse-Player," *Southern Review* 9 (October 1973): 828–56.

23. "To Remind You of July," *House and Garden*, December 1923, 51; "A New Hampshire House and Garden," *House and Garden*, March 1924, 75–77.

24. Shipman, "List of Annual Seeds for Autumn Planting for Brook Place," in Blue Book, summer 1930 (Streeter collection).

CHAPTER SIX
Artistic Maturity

1. *Garden Magazine,* July 1923, 319, and June 1924, 268; *House and Garden,* October 1923, 65; *House Beautiful,* March 1924, 256.

2. About one hundred titles from Shipman's library were donated in 1974 to the Avery Architectural Library, Columbia University, New York.

3. According to Dan Kiley, who worked for Warren Manning from 1932 to 1938, Shipman and Manning were friends. He remembered seeing her in Manning's office more than once. Dan Kiley, telephone interview with Robin Karson, 15 June 1995.

4. Shipman, letter to Mrs. Windsor T. White, 11 February 1942 (box 8, folder 35, Cornell); Marie Daerr, "Arts and Flowers," *Cleveland Press,* 18 April 1941; "Ellen Shipman Coming to Discuss Group of Different Gardens," *Your Garden and Home* (Cleveland), March 1941, 11, 20–21; Mac Griswold and Eleanor Weller, *The Golden Age of American Gardens* (New York: Harry N. Abrams/Garden Club of America, 1991), 283.

5. Griswold and Weller, *Golden Age,* 78.

6. Sparks, "Landscape Architect Discusses Gardens," 20, 70–71.

7. Current owner of estate, interview with author, 23 June 1994.

8. Ethel B. Power, "A Blue-Ribbon Garden: The Garden of Mrs. Holden McGinley," *House Beautiful,* March 1933, 88.

9. This fountain was also used in the Eugene du Pont garden in Wilmington, Del.; its price was $1,500.

10. Kate Brewster, *The Little Garden for Little Money* (Boston: Atlantic Monthly Press, 1924); Mrs. Francis King, *From a New Garden* (New York, Alfred A. Knopf, 1928), 12–13. I am indebted to Virginia Lopez Begg for the latter reference.

11. Mrs. Francis King, "An English Country Place in Michigan," *Country Life in America,* April 1928, 59.

CHAPTER SEVEN
The Border

1. Shipman, letter to William D. Conner, 12 June 1936 (U.S. Military Academy, West Point, archives).

2. Shipman, letter to Clara Ford, Dearborn, Mich., 3 June 1930 (box 37, Fair Lane Papers). The Fords may have recommended Shipman to Thomas A. Edison, in Lewellyn Park, N.J., for whom she also did a garden, but the design and dates of her work there escaped documentation.

3. Manning, letter to Gertrude Seiberling, Akron, Ohio, 19 January 1916; Manning, letter to Frank Seiberling, Akron, Ohio, 7 March 1916 (Stan Hywet).

4. Manning, letter to Frank Seiberling, Akron, Ohio, 20 July 1917; Manning report, 20 April 1928; Manning, "Report on the Estate of Mr. Frank A. Seiberling, Akron, Ohio," typescript, 7 November 1928 (Stan Hywet).

5. Harrison-Karson interview.

6. M. Christine Doell and Gerald Doell, "Restoration of the English Garden Plantings at Stan Hywet Hall," report, January 1991, 9 (Stan Hywet); Shipman, letter to Clara Ford, Dearborn, Mich., 3 June 1930 (box 37, Fair Lane).

CHAPTER EIGHT
A Grander Scope

1. Christie-Vernon interview transcript, 2.

2. "The Garden in Good Taste: The Garden of Carll Tucker, Esq.," *House Beautiful*, October 1928, 388–91.

3. "To Link the Lawns and Garden," *House and Garden*, August 1930, 49, 55–57.

4. Shipman, letter to Mrs. R. F. Willingham, Atlanta, Ga., 23 April 1945 (box 8, folder 27, Cornell).

5. Adaline D. Piper, "The Charm of Chatham," *House Beautiful*, April 1926, 437–38.

6. Now part of the Fredericksburg National Military Park, the garden underwent preservation treatment by the National Park Service in the 1980s which focused on stabilizing Shipman's garden walls and structures and restoring the parterre. Reed Engle, interview with author, 6 September 1994.

7. In a rare bit of British publicity, Shipman was hailed by London *Garden Design* as "one of the best known landscape architects in the United States, ... noted for her use of the formal garden, when closely related to the house, as well as her naturalistic development of the whole place." Alice Bourquin and Jessie Bourquin, "The Formal in American Gardens," *Garden Design* (London) 17 (1934): 104.

8. For more on the topic, see Harold Donaldson Eberlein, "The Cotswold Influence in America," *Country Life in America*, June 1921, 58–60.

9. Notation on reverse of small snapshot of Snowshill included in Salvage file (box 5, envelope 32, Cornell).

10. Giles Edgerton, "Cotswold Again Influences American Architecture," *Arts and Decoration*, June 1937, 20.

CHAPTER NINE
Wild Gardens

1. "Variety of Form and Abundance of Bloom within a Small Area: The Garden of Mrs. Henry V. Greenough, Brookline, Massachusetts," *House Beautiful*, March 1931, 62.

2. Design chapter, GNB, 50.

3. Shipman's notation on the reverse of a snapshot taken at the Clapp project— "brook from which we got the stone"—offers proof of her willingness to "reinvent" nature (box 1, envelope 40, Cornell).

4. Melanie Fleischmann, "Long Live Longue Vue," *House Beautiful,* July 1994, 34-38.

5. Design chapter, GNB, 50.

CHAPTER TEN
The Great Depression and the Lure of Europe

1. Louis E. Shipman obituary, *New York Times,* 3 August 1933.

2. At various points Shipman worked for the Gordon, James, P. Huber, Ralph, and Robert Haneses, as well as the Chatham and Knox families, who were related by marriage.

3. DeWitt Hanes quoted in Mac Griswold, "Carolina Grown," *House and Garden,* September 1988, 181.

4. *Winston-Salem Journal,* 8 October 1932; Griswold, "Carolina Grown."

5. Lois Byrd, "Landscaper, at 72, Takes a New Job," *Louisville (Ky.) Courier-Journal,* 5 November 1942.

6. *Boston Herald,* 27 October 1935 (Colby collection).

7. Harry G. Healy, letter to Shipman, 15 July 1935; Shipman, letter to Healy, 22 July 1935 (box 10, folder 7, Cornell).

8. Design chapter, GNB, 56.

9. The interior of the Michigan house featured one of the country's outstanding private collections of eighteenth-century art, assembled by Joseph Duveen. See Hawkins Ferry, "Mansions of Grosse Pointe: A Suburb in Good Taste," *Michigan Society of Architects Journal,* March 1956.

10. Notation on reverse of photograph (box 6, envelope 11, Cornell).

11. Edith Stern, interview with Pamela Bardo, 3 July 1977, typescript, 1–2 (file, Longue Vue).

12. Shipman, telegram to Mrs. Edgar Stern, 3 July 1946 (Longue Vue).

13. Stern-Bardo interview typescript, 6.

14. Ibid., 3.

15. Edith Stern took the opportunity to transform the classical French vista into a Spanish court, having recently visited the Generalife garden of the Alhambra. William Platt assisted with the new design.

CHAPTER ELEVEN
Public and Institutional Projects

1. Shipman, letter to Willingham.

2. The grounds were severely damaged by the hurricane of 1938; later additions to the building and the encroachment of I-84 reduced the acreage. For a description of the roof garden, see "Flowers Look Down on Tallest Trees from Aetna's Wonderland in the Air," *Hartford Courant,* 1 June 1952.

3. Mary Jane Carbonara, "The Evolution of the Sarah P. Duke Gardens at Duke University," course paper, Duke University, 1978 (Duke University Archives).

4. Marcus Embry, "Watching the Gardens Grow: The Sarah P. Duke Gardens: A Botanical Birthday," *Duke Magazine,* July–August 1989, 8.

5. After the war, when the gardens needed rejuvenation, Shipman was asked to advise but noted that the new gardener was loath to follow her suggestions and complained, "It is like leaving a baby on a doorstep—I just can't let one of my gardens go without developing it as it should be." Shipman, letter to T. L. Perkins, New York City, 12 April 1946 (box 9, folder 11, Cornell).

6. Shipman, letter to Willingham.

CHAPTER TWELVE
Last Years

1. Byrd, "Landscaper, at 72, Takes a New Job"; "Drive That Nail," *Laurel (Miss.) Leader-Call,* undated clipping (box 10, folder 7, Cornell).

2. Shipman, letter to Charles Meyette, Plainfield, N.H., 18 September 1945 (box 8, folder 12, Cornell).

3. Dona E. Caldwell, interview with author, 6 September 1994; Shipman, correspondence with Charles Meyette and others, 1945–46 (box 8, folder 12, Cornell); Caldwell, letter to author, 29 December 1993.

4. Anne Bruce Haldeman, letter to John H. Dryfhout, 12 September 1984 (Saint-Gaudens National Historic Site).

5. Haldeman worked on the book as late as 1958. Introductory pages from the manuscript resurfaced in 1984, when Catherine Zusy received the outline and prefaces from Haldeman and sent copies of this material to Saint-Gaudens National Historic Site, where they can be examined today. The remainder of the manuscript and Shipman's working notes were located by the author in September 1994 and are presently being prepared for publication.

6. Preface no. 2, GNB, 1.

7. Shipman, letter to Aymar Embury II, New York City, 6 May 1946 (box 9, folder 7, Cornell).

8. McCormic–Van Buren interview, transcript, 6.

9. Diana Kostial McGuire, letter to Robin Karson, Amherst, Mass., 18 November 1994.

10. Shipman, letter to Henry S. Walker, Evansville, Ind., 20 December 1946 (box 9, folder 14, Cornell); Shipman, letter to Edith Stern, 11 July 1947 (box 8, folder 58, Cornell).

11. Barbara Johnstone, letter to author, 5 November 1994.

12. Shipman, letter to Gertrude Kuh, 4 March 1946 (courtesy of Betsy Fitzsimmons).

13. Shipman, letter to Edith Stern, 26 February 1950 (box 8, folder 58, Cornell).

EPILOGUE

1. Will, 9 November 1948, Newport Probate Office, Newport, N.H.

2. Correspondence between Shipman's office and Hubert B. Owens, Head, Department of Landscape Architecture, University of Georgia, Athens, 22 April to 2 May 1946 (box 9, folder 11, Cornell).

SELECT BIBLIOGRAPHY

MANUSCRIPT RESOURCES

Main Repositories

Cornell University, Ithaca, N.Y. Ellen Shipman Collection, file no. 1259, Rare and Manuscript Collections, Carl A. Kroch Library. Approximately four thousand plans and drawings, five hundred photographs, correspondence, clippings, Garden Note Book (partial copy). The collection represents nearly three hundred projects. A catalog is available. Cited in notes as Cornell.

Archives of American Gardens, Horticultural Services Division, Arts and Industries Building, Room 2282, Smithsonian Institution, Washington, D.C. Slides of Shipman gardens.

Dona E. Caldwell Private Collection, Fairfield, Conn. Eleven projects associated with Agnes Selkirk Clark (some duplicates from Cornell).

Long Island Studies Institute, Nassau County Museum, 619 Fulton Avenue, Hempstead, N.Y. Collection of Mattie Edwards Hewitt photographs of Long Island commissions.

Society for the Preservation of Long Island Antiquities, 93 North Country Road, Setauket, N.Y. Information on Long Island commissions.

Nancy Streeter Private Collection, New York, N.Y. Correspondence, photographs, memorabilia.

University of Oregon, Eugene, Ore. Lord and Schryver Collection no. 98, files 87–89, Special Collections, Knight Library. Plans only; twenty-five projects associated with Edith Schryver.

Other Repositories

Local libraries and historical societies (Greenwich, Conn., and Grosse Pointe, Mich., for instance) have additional information. Private owners of extant Shipman gardens occasionally have plans, photographs, and correspondence. In addition, the following institutions have information on Shipman commissions (client name in brackets) or related material.

Dartmouth College, Hanover, N.H. Special Collections, Baker Library. Diaries, photographs, memorabilia relating to Cornish Colony. Cited in notes as Dartmouth.

Duke University, Durham, N.C. University Archives has photographs, reports, and correspondence. [Duke]

Fredericksburg and Spotsylvania National Military Park, 120 Chatham Lane, Fredericksburg, Va. Plans and photographs, small exhibition on view. [Devore]

Gwinn Estate, 12407 Lake Shore Boulevard, Bratenahl, Ohio. Plans, photographs, correspondence. [Mather]

Henry Ford Museum and Research Center, 20900 Oakwood Blvd., Dearborn, Mich. Correspondence, blueprints, photographs in Fair Lane Papers. Cited in notes as Fair Lane Papers. [Ford]

Longue Vue Gardens, 7 Bamboo Road, New Orleans, La. Plans, correspondence, photographs in archives. Cited in notes as Longue Vue. [Stern]

Philip Read Memorial Library, Plainfield, N.H. Plan for Plainfield School.

Plainfield Historical Society, Plainfield, N.H. Photographs of Brook Place, memorabilia, hand-colored glass slides from annual garden contests.

Saint-Gaudens National Historic Site, Cornish, N.H. Artwork and photographs relating to Cornish Colony; Garden Note Book (partial copy). Cited in notes as Saint-Gaudens.

Stan Hywet Hall and Gardens, 714 North Portage Path, Akron, Ohio. Plans, photographs, correspondence in archives. Cited in notes as Stan Hywet. [Seiberling]

SECONDARY SOURCES

Following is a selection of references to Ellen Shipman's work as well as noteworthy general studies on the Country Place Era. Known regional publications and newspaper references have been cited, but a complete listing has not been possible. Mattie Edwards Hewitt supplied photographs of architecture, gardens, and interiors to *McCalls, Town and Country, Vogue,* and other popular periodicals, which may provide additional sources of information. The name of the relevant client is given in brackets.

Anner, Rosemarie T. "The Golden Age of Landscaping: Digging Up the Past," *Greenwich* 47 (May 1994): 56–76. [Croft, Mitchell]

Baker, John Cordes, ed. *American Country Houses and Their Gardens.* Philadelphia: John C. Winston/House and Garden, 1906. 134–37. [Platt]

Barnstone, Howard. *The Architecture of John F. Staub: Houston and the South.* Austin: University of Texas Press, 1979. [Farish, Hogg]

Bedford, Stephen, and Richard Guy Wilson. *The Long Island Country House, 1870–1930.* Exh. cat. Southampton, N.Y.: Parrish Art Museum, 1988.

Biddle, Ellen McGowan. *Recollections.* Boston: Small, Maynard, 1920.

_____. *Reminiscences of a Soldier's Wife.* Philadelphia: J. B. Lippincott, 1907.

Birnbaum, Charles, and Lisa Crowder, eds. *Pioneers of American Landscape Design.* Washington, D.C.: National Park Service/Preservation Assistance Division, 1993.

Bloom, Ann. "Ellen Biddle Shipman." Paper written for Radcliffe Seminars Landscape Design Program, 1986.

Bourquin, Alice, and Jessie Bourquin. "The Formal in American Gardens," *Garden Design* (London) 17 (1934): 104–6. [Newberry, Sales]

Briggs, Martha, et al. *Long Island Estate Gardens.* Exh. cat. Greenvale, N.Y.: Long Island University, 1985. [Kramer, Lord, Salvage]

Brower, Carol Ann. "Tregaron: Form and Transformation of an American Villa." M.L.A. thesis, Cornell University, 1986. [Parmelee]

Brown, Catherine R. "Women and the Land: A Biographical Survey of Women Who Have Contributed to the Development of Landscape Architecture in the United States." Morgan State University Built Environment Studies, Baltimore, 1979.

Bullard, Roger H. "A House Especially Designed for the Dunes of East Hampton," *Arts and Decoration,* October 1929, 68–69, 112, 170. [James]

Bush-Brown, Louise, and James Bush-Brown. "Laverock Hill: The Garden of Mr. and Mrs. Issac T. Starr at Chestnut Hill," in *Portraits of Philadelphia Gardens.* Philadelphia: Dorrance, 1929.

Byrd, Lois. "Landscaper, at 72, Takes a New Job," *Louisville (Ky.) Courier-Journal,* 5 November 1942.

Cane, Percy, ed. *Modern Gardens British and Foreign.* London: The Studio/Special Winter Number, 1926–27, 102. [Croft]

Caparn, Harold A. "Garden Paths and How to Make Them," *Arts and Decoration*, April 1937, 29. [Bulkley]

Carbonara, Mary Jane. "The Evolution of the Sarah P. Duke Gardens at Duke University: The Growth of an Aesthetic Institution." Paper written for Department of Landscape Architecture, Duke University, 1978.

Close, Leslie Rose. "Ellen Biddle Shipman," in *American Landscape Architecture: Designers and Places*, edited by William Tishler. Washington, D.C.: Preservation Press, 1989.

_____. *Portrait of an Era in Landscape Architecture: The Photographs of Mattie Edwards Hewitt.* Exh. cat. Bronx, N.Y.: Wave Hill, 1983.

"A Connecticut House with a Southern Accent," *House and Garden*, July 1949, 70–71.

Cortissoz, Royal. "Charles Adams Platt, 1861–1933, An Appreciation," *Architecture* 68 (November 1922): 271.

_____. *Domestic Architecture of H. T. Lindeberg.* New York: William Helburn, 1940.

Crawford, Mary Caroline. "Homes and Gardens of Cornish," *House Beautiful*, April 1906, 12–14.

Croly, Herbert D. "The Architectural Work of Charles A. Platt," *Architectural Record* 15 (March 1904): 181–242.

_____. "English Renaissance at Its Best. The House of James Parmelee at Washington, D.C., Charles A. Platt, Architect," *Architectural Record* 36 (August 1914): 81–97.

_____. "A Waterfront Villa. The House of Russell A. Alger, Jr.," *Architectural Record* 36 (December 1914): 481–86.

Cummin, Hazel E. "What Constitutes a Good Garden? The Garden of Mr. and Mrs. George Meade in Dayton, Ohio, Answers This Question," *House Beautiful*, March 1931, 241–45.

Cunningham, Mary P. "Design in Planting," *House Beautiful*, October 1924, 320, 323, 324. [Kramer]

_____. "Notes from Some Virginia Gardens," *House Beautiful*, August 1930, 164, 179–80. [Devore]

Daerr, Marie. "Arts and Flowers," *Cleveland Press*, 18 April 1941, 29.

"Design in a Michigan Garden," *House and Garden*, September 1926, 108–9. [McGraw]

Dryfhout, John H. "The Gardens of Augustus Saint-Gaudens," *House and Garden*, December 1985, 144–48, 199.

_____, et al. *A Circle of Friends: Art Colonies of Cornish and Dublin.* Exh. cat. Durham, N.H.: University Art Galleries, 1985.

Duncan, Frances. "The Gardens of Cornish," *Century Magazine*, May 1906, 3–19. [Poins House]

Eberlein, Harold Donaldson. "The Cotswold Influence in America," *Country Life in America*, June 1921, 58–60.

Edgell, G. H. *The American Architecture of To-Day.* New York: Charles Scribner's Sons, 1928. [Brook Place]

Edgerton, Giles. "Cotswold Again Influences American Architecture," *Arts and Decoration*, June 1937, 20–22. [Mitchell]

"The Edging Plant in Herbaceous Gardens," *House Beautiful*, July 1925, 34, 73. [Croft]

"Ellen Shipman Coming to Discuss Group of Different Gardens," *Your Garden and Home* (Cleveland), March 1941, 11, 20–21.

Elwood, P. H., Jr., ed. *American Landscape Architecture.* New York: Architectural Book Publishing, 1924. [Brewster, Croft, Parmelee, Smith]

Embry, Marcus. "Watching the Gardens Grow: The Sarah P. Duke Gardens: A Botanical Birthday," *Duke Magazine*, July–August 1989, 6–11.

Embury, Aymar, II. "Charles A. Platt—His Work," *Architecture* 26 (August 1912): 130–62.

Evans, Catherine. *Cultural Landscape Report for Longfellow National Historic Site.* Vol. 1. Boston: National Park Service, 1993. [Longfellow]

Famous Gardens Selected from Country Life. New York: Country Life/American Home Corporation, 1937. [Bacon, Salvage]

Fenelon, Eunice. "Open House in the Gardens of Greater Cleveland," *Your Garden and Home* (Cleveland), June 1934, 13, 20. [White]

Ferry, Hawkins. "Mansions of Grosse Pointe: A Suburb in Good Taste." Reprint from *Michigan Society of Architects Journal,* March 1956.

Fitch, James M., and F. F. Rockwell. *Treasury of American Gardens.* New York: Harper and Brothers, 1956. [Kanzler, Mather]

Fleischmann, Melanie. "Long Live Longue Vue," *House Beautiful,* July 1994, 34–38. [Stern]

"Flower Time in Two Gardens at Grosse Pointe," *Garden Magazine and Home Builder,* April 1928, 165. [Brewster]

"A Focal Point for the Garden," *House and Garden,* January 1927, 69. [White]

"Four Views of the Garden at Estate of William Fahnestock, Esq., Katonah, New York," *Journal of the International Garden Club* 2 (September 1918): 361–64.

Frary, I. T. "Residence of Mr. and Mrs. Willard M. Clapp, Cleveland Heights, Ohio," *Architectural Record* 62 (October 1927): 273–80.

"Fynmere, the Garden of Mr. James Fenimore Cooper, Cooperstown, N.Y.," *Country Life in America,* undated tearsheet, courtesy Catherine Zusy.

"Fynmere, the House of James Fenimore Cooper, Esq., Frank P. Whiting, Architect," *Architectural Record* 30 (October 1911): 360–68.

"A Garden by the Sea," *House Beautiful,* March 1930, 290–91. [Alger]

"The Garden in Good Taste," *House Beautiful,* August 1923, 132. [Croft]

"The Garden in Good Taste, the Garden of Carll Tucker, Esq.," *House Beautiful,* October 1928, 388–91.

"The Garden in Good Taste, the Garden of Miss Mary Pruyn, East Hampton, Long Island," *House Beautiful,* March 1924, 236, 253–56.

"The Garden of A. L. Kramer, Esq., Westbury, Long Island," *House Beautiful,* March 1924, 255.

"The Garden of James Fenimore Cooper at Cooperstown, New York," *House Beautiful,* July 1924, 30–31.

"The Garden of Mr. and Mrs. Edwin Scott Barbour," *House Beautiful,* June 1930, 738–40.

"The Garden of Mrs. A. L. Kramer at Westbury, L.I.," *Garden Magazine,* April 1924, 128–29.

"The Garden of Mrs. C. Suydam Cutting at Gladstone, N.J.," *Country Life in America,* June 1933, 42–43.

"The Garden of Mrs. Robert A. Franks, Orange, New Jersey," *House Beautiful,* August 1926, 166–67.

"The Garden of Samuel Morris, Esq., in Chestnut Hill, Pennsylvania," *House Beautiful,* July 1927, 30–31.

Garden Magazine, April 1923, 101. [Croft] June 1923, 238. [Croft] July 1923, 319. [Magee] August 1923, 361. [Croft] October 1923, 71, 73, 75, 92–93. [Pruyn, Kramer, Brewster] June 1924, 268, 269, 279. [Brewster, Croft, Magee]

Garden Magazine and Home Builder, September 1924, 11. [Morris] October 1924, 91. [Gossler] February 1926, 433. [Starr] March 1926, 25. [Starr] September 1926, 29, 41. [Starr] November 1926, 204. [Starr] July 1927, 486. [Reeves] September 1927, 44. [Starr]

"A Garden Which Looks Well All Year," *House and Garden,* December 1949, 140–41. [Spalding]

"The Gardener's Calendar for July," *House and Garden,* July 1923, 76.

Gardens and Gardening 1939. London: The Studio, 1939, 45. [Tucker]

Gardens and Gardening 1940. London: The Studio, 1940. [de Waal, McGinley, Tucker]

"The Gardens of H. W. Croft, Greenwich, Ct." *House and Garden,* March 1923, 54–55, 57.

Griswold, Mac. "Carolina Grown," *House and Garden,* September 1988, 176–83. [Hanes]

Griswold, Mac, and Eleanor Weller. *The Golden Age of American Gardens: Proud Owners, Private Estates, 1890–1940.* New York: Harry N. Abrams/Garden Club of America, 1991. [Alger, Brewster, Brown, Devore, Franks, Kellogg, Neff, Parmelee, Schley, Starr, Stern, White]

Haldeman, Anne Bruce, and Louise Leland, "In Vermont Hills, Mr. and Mrs. Horace Brown," *House Beautiful,* June 1934, 40–43, 79. [Brown]

Hefner, Robert J., Clay Lancaster, and Robert A. M. Stern. *East Hampton's Heritage: An Illustrated Architectural Record.* New York: W. W. Norton, 1982. [James, Maidstone Club]

Henke, Ellen. "Garden Destinations: Longue Vue Gardens," *Flower and Garden,* December 1992/January 1993, 18–23. [Stern]

Hewitt, Mark Alan. *The Architect and the American Country House, 1890–1940.* New Haven: Yale University Press, 1990.

"An Historic House Regains Its Youth," *House and Garden,* May 1934, 55–57. [F. Pratt]

Hopkins, Alfred. "An Architect Turns Client," *House and Garden,* November 1933, 24, 62.

"House and Garden's Own Hall of Fame," *House and Garden,* June 1933, 50.

"A House in New Canaan, Connecticut," *House Beautiful,* January 1924, 41. [Gossler]

"House of Alfred Hopkins, Architect, Princeton, New Jersey," *Architecture* 68 (November 1933): 273–82.

"House of Philip Gossler, Wheatley Hills, Long Island," *Architecture* 54 (December 1926): 383–88.

"House of Samuel A. Salvage, Glen Head, Long Island," *Architecture* 59 (June 1929): 359–66.

Howe, Samuel. *American Country Houses of To-Day.* New York: Architectural Book Publishing, 1915. [Alger, Brewster, Jennings, Parmelee]

"In a Long Island Garden," *House and Garden,* October 1926, 129. [Schmidlapp]

"In a Michigan Garden," *House and Garden,* March 1927, 88–91. [Sales]

"In Memoriam," *Garden Club of America Bulletin,* July 1950, 1.

Karr, Gerald. *Historic Structure Report [for] Chatham.* Denver: U.S. Department of the Interior, 1984. [Devore]

Karson, Robin. *The Muses of Gwinn: Art and Nature in a Garden Designed by Warren H. Manning, Charles A. Platt, and Ellen Biddle Shipman.* New York: Sagapress/Library of American Landscape History, 1995.

Keefe, Charles S., ed. *The American House.* New York: U. P. C. Book, 1922. [Mitchell]

Kenworthy, Richard. *The Italian Garden Transplanted: Renaissance Revival Landscape Design in America, 1850–1939.* Exh. cat. Troy, Ala.: Troy State University, 1988.

King, Mrs. Francis. "An English Country Place in Michigan," *Country Life in America,* April 1928, 58–60. [Lowe]

Knight, Jane A. "An Examination of the History of the Lowthorpe School of Landscape Architecture for Women." M.L.A. thesis, Cornell University, 1986.

Krall, Daniel W. "Early Women Designers and Their Work in Public Places," in *Proceedings for Landscapes and Gardens: Women Who Made a Difference,* edited by Miriam Easton Rutz. East Lansing: Michigan State University, June 1987.

_____. "Ellen Biddle Shipman and Her Design for Longue Vue Gardens." Paper presented at conference of Council of Educators in Landscape Architecture, St. Amelia's Island, September 1989.

_____. "Ellen Biddle Shipman: Dean of Women Landscape Architects." Manuscript, Department of Landscape Architecture, Cornell University, undated.

_____. "Ellen Biddle Shipman: Dean of Women Landscape Architects." Paper presented at Masters of American Garden Design symposium, PaineWebber and American Horticultural Society, New York, January 1990.

_____. "A Half Century of Garden Design: The Drawings of Landscape Architect Ellen Shipman." Exh. notes. Ithaca, N.Y., Hartell Gallery, Cornell University, April 1986.

Krider, Karen. "Ellen Biddle Shipman," in _Pioneers of American Landscape Design_, edited by Charles Birnbaum and Lisa Crowder. Washington, D.C.: National Park Service/Preservation Assistance Division, 1993.

_____. "Ellen Biddle Shipman's Planting Design Focusing on Stan Hywet Gardens." M.L.A thesis, University of Oregon, 1995. [Seiberling]

Kummen, Merle, S. Zimmerman, and R. Pawlowski. _Hartford Architecture_. Vol 3. Hartford: Hartford Architectural Conservancy, 1980. [Aetna]

Lay, Charles Downing. "An Interview with Charles A. Platt," _Landscape Architecture_ 2 (April 1912): 127–31.

Leong, William B. S. "University Gardens: A Development Plan," _Landscape Architecture_ 50 (Autumn 1959): 35–44. [Duke]

Levy, David W. _Herbert Croly of "The New Republic": The Life and Thought of an American Progressive_. Princeton: Princeton University Press, 1985.

Lockwood, Alice G. B., ed. _Gardens of Colony and State_. New York: Charles Scribner's Sons/ Garden Club of America, 1931, 1934. [Grosse Pointe Gardens]

"Long Island Shows a Varied Garden," _House and Garden_, October 1936, 89. [Salvage]

"Looking over the Garden Wall," _Country Life in America_, March 1917, 68–69. [Parmelee]

Lowell, Guy, ed. _American Gardens_. Boston: Bates and Guild, 1902. [Cornish gardens]

McCormick, Kathleen. "In the Path of the Setting Sun: The Gardens at Henry Ford's Fair Lane," _Historic Preservation_, May–June 1995, 86–91, 125.

_____. "On a Clear Day: Akron's Stan Hywet Restores Its American-Style Landscape," _Historic Preservation_, July–August 1994, 68–69, 99–103. [Seiberling]

"Magnificently Done in Chagrin Falls: The Ohio Estate of Mr. and Mrs. E. S. Burke, Jr.," _Country Life in America_, March 1937, 65–66.

Meador, Deborah Kay. "The Making of a Landscape Architect: Ellen Biddle Shipman and Her Years at the Cornish Art Colony." M.L.A. thesis, Cornell University, 1989.

Miller, Wilhelm. "An 'Italian Garden' That Is Full of Flowers," _Country Life in America_, March 1905, 485.

Mitchell, Evelyn Scott. "Longue Vue: A Short History of the Gardens." Manuscript, Longue Vue Gardens, New Orleans. [Stern]

"A Modernist Garden Appears in America," _House and Garden_, November 1929, 105. [Clapp]

Monograph on the Work of Charles A. Platt. Introduction by Royal Cortissoz. New York: Architectural Book Publishing, 1913.

Morgan, Keith N. _Charles A. Platt: The Artist as Architect_. Cambridge and New York: MIT Press/Architectural History Foundation, 1985.

_____. "Charles A. Platt's Houses and Gardens in Cornish, New Hampshire," _Antiques_, July 1982, 117–29.

"Mrs. Ellen Shipman, Landscape Designer." Obituary. _New York Times_, 29 March 1950.

"Mrs. Ellen Shipman, Famous Landscape Architect, Thrills Hearers," _Winston-Salem Journal_, 8 October 1932.

"Mrs. Robert Brewster's Garden at Mt. Kisco, New York," *Garden Magazine,* October 1923, 75, 92–93.

Murray, Pauline. *Planning and Planting the Home Garden.* New York: Orange Judd Publishing, 1932. [Pruyn]

Nevins, Deborah. "The Triumph of Flora: Women and the American Landscape, 1890–1935," *Antiques,* April 1985, 904–22.

"A New Hampshire House and Garden," *House and Garden,* March 1924, 75–77. [Brook Place]

"New Jersey Follows Spain in a Garden within Patio Walls," *House and Garden,* August 1930, 49, 55–57. [Schley]

Nichols, Rose Standish. "A Hilltop Garden in New Hampshire," *House Beautiful,* March 1934, 237–39, 290.

Noble, William. "Northcote: An Artist's New Hampshire Garden," *Journal of the New England Garden History Society* 2 (1992): 1–9.

Norwalk, Nancy, and Harold Zea, eds. *Choice White Pines and Good Land: A History of Plainfield and Meriden, New Hampshire.* Portsmouth, N.H.: Peter E. Randall, 1991.

"Old English Magnificiently Done in Chagrin Falls," *Country Life in America,* March 1937, 64–69. [Burke]

Patterson, Augusta Owen. *American Homes of To-Day, Their Architectural Style, Their Environment, Their Characteristics.* New York: Macmillan, 1924. [Brewster, Lord]

_____. "Mrs. Robert Bacon's Westbury Garden," *Town and Country,* August 1926, 44–47.

"Paved Pools Add the Final Terrace Touch," *House and Garden,* May 1933, 44. [Godley]

Perrett, Antoinette. "A Rose and Purple Garden in July," *House Beautiful,* July 1922, 21, 72. [Abbott]

Petersen, Anne. "Women Take the Lead in Landscape Art," *New York Times,* 13 March 1938.

Piper, Adaline D. "The Charm of Chatham," *House Beautiful,* April 1926, 437–41. [Devore]

"Planting That Reflects the Natural Surroundings: The Estate of Mr. and Mrs. Allan Wood," House Beautiful, August 1931, 130–32.

Platt, Charles A. *Italian Gardens.* 1894. Reprint, with an overview by Keith N. Morgan. New York: Sagapress/Timber Press, 1993.

"A Pool for Every Garden," *House and Garden,* June 1920, 26. [Mitchell]

Power, Ethel B. "A Blue-Ribbon Garden: The Garden of Mrs. Holden McGinley," *House Beautiful,* March 1933, 86–89, 118–19.

Pratt, Richard H. "Gardens Adorned and Negligee," *House and Garden,* June 1924, 54–55. [Croft]

Pressley, Marion, and Cynthia Zaitzevsky. *Cultural Landscape Report for Saint-Gaudens National Historic Site.* Boston: National Park Service, 1993.

Randall, Monica. *The Mansions of Long Island's Gold Coast.* New York: Rizzoli, 1987. [Kramer]

Rehmann, Elsa. *Garden-Making.* Boston: Houghton Mifflin, 1926. [Abbott, Magee, Mitchell]

"Residence of Grenville T. Emmet, New York," *Architectural Record* 46 (November 1919): 476–83.

Russell, Elizabeth H. "A House on Beekman Place," *House Beautiful,* November 1927, 512–16, 568–69. [Shipman]

"Rynwood, House of Samuel A. Salvage, Esq.," *Architectural Forum* 53 (July 1930): 51–85.

Sale, Edith Tunis. *Historic Gardens of Virginia.* Revised edition. Richmond: James River Garden Club, 1930. [Devore]

Sclare, Lisa, and Donald Sclare. *Beaux-Arts Estates: A Guide to the Architecture of Long Island.* New York: Viking Press, 1980. [Gossler, Hutton]

Sexton, R. W. "A House and Garden in Suburban New Jersey," *Arts and Decoration,* February 1937, 14–15, 49. [Foster]

Shelton, Louise. *Beautiful Gardens in America*. New York: Charles Scribner's Sons, 1915. [Merrill]
_____. *Beautiful Gardens in America*. Revised edition. New York: Charles Scribner's Sons, 1924. [Abbott, Brewster, Croft, Morris, Smith, Starr]

Shipman, Ellen. "How I Teach My Own Children," *Ladies Home Journal*, September 1911, 60.
_____. "Rhymes of Bermuda," *Garden Club of America Bulletin*, March 1933, 54.
_____. "The Saint-Gaudens Memorial Gardens," *Garden Club of America Bulletin*, May 1948, 61–65.
_____. "Window Gardens for Little Money," *Ladies Home Journal*, September 1911, 30.

"Some Garden Pictures," *House Beautiful*, July 1923, 45. [Croft]

"Some Philadelphia and Wilmington Gardens," *Landscape Architecture* 28 (April 1938): 123. [Starr]

"Southern Colonial," *Country Life in America*, January 1937, 30. [Stern]

Sparks, Lamar. "A Landscape Architect Discusses Gardens," *Better Homes and Gardens*, November 1930, 20, 70–71.

Steele, Fletcher, ed. *House Beautiful Gardening Manual*. Boston: Atlantic Monthly, 1926. [Brewster, Cooper, Daniels, Franks, Pruyn]

Stern, Robert A. M., Gregory Gilmartin, and Thomas Mellins. *New York 1930: Architecture and Urbanism between Two World Wars*. New York: Rizzoli, 1987. [Beekman Place]

Stone, Doris M. "Longue Vue," *American Horticulturist*, June 1987, 28–31.

Tankard, Judith B. "Women Pioneers in Landscape Design," *Radcliffe Quarterly* 79 (March 1993): 8–11.

"Three Pages of Charming Gardens," *House and Garden*, October 1923, 65. [Magee]

"Three Pennsylvania Gardens, *Garden Magazine and Home Builder*, September 1924, 11. [Morris]

"To Link the Lawns and Garden," *House and Garden*, August 1930, 49, 55–57. [Schley]

"To Remind You of July," *House and Garden*, December 1923, 51. [Brook Place]

Town and Country, 1 February 1927, 47–51. [Gossler]

"Two Gardens at Mount Kisco, New York," *House Beautiful*, March 1924, 256. [Brewster, Magee]

"Use Pattern in a Vista," *House and Garden*, March 1951, 167. [Kanzler]

Van Buren, Deborah E. "The Cornish Colony: Expressions of Attachment to Place, 1885–1915." Ph.D. diss., George Washington University, May 1987.
_____. "Landscape Architecture and Gardens in the Cornish Colony: The Careers of Rose Nichols, Ellen Shipman, and Frances Duncan," *Women's Studies* 14 (September 1988): 367–88.
_____. "Women and Landscape Architecture: Rose Nichols and Ellen Shipman in the Cornish Colony." Paper presented at the annual meeting of the American Studies Association, San Diego, October 1985.

Van Horn, Henry. "Mr. A. L. Kramer's Residence at Westbury," *Town and Country*, 1 May 1920, 53–56.

"Variety of Form and Abundance of Bloom within a Small Area: The Garden of Mrs. Henry V. Greenough, Brookline, Massachusetts," *House Beautiful*, March 1931, 259–62.

Wade, Hugh Mason. *A Brief History of Cornish, 1763–1974*. Hanover, N.H.: University Press of New England, 1976.

Warren, Bonnie. "Longue Vue: A Tribute to Classical Tradition in New Orleans," *Southern Accents*, September–October 1985, 72, 79. [Stern]

Warren, Dale. "The Garden as a Frame for the House," *House Beautiful*, October 1926, 426–27. [Brook Place]

"Weeping Cherry for Spring Enchantment," *House and Garden,* March 1941, 16. [Williams].

"When It's Spring in an Ohio Garden," *House and Garden,* May 1929, 111–13. [Clapp]

White, Edward, "Garden Design," *Journal of the International Garden Club* 1 (August 1917): 45. [Hegeman]

Wright, Richardson, ed. *House and Garden's Book of Gardens.* New York: Condé Nast, 1921. [Abbott, Mitchell, Parmelee]

_____. *House and Garden's Second Book of Gardens.* New York: Condé Nast, 1927. [Croft, Sales, White]

Yearbook of the Architectural League of New York, 1923. [Croft, Magee]

Yearbook of the Architectural League of New York, 1929. [Salvage]

Zusy, Catherine. "A Unity of Design in the American Spirit: James Fenimore Cooper II's 'Fynmere.'" Paper written for the Cooperstown [N.Y.] History Museum Studies Program, 1984.

AUTHOR'S ACKNOWLEDGMENTS

WHEN THE INVITATION came from the Library of American Landscape History to prepare Shipman's biography, I welcomed the opportunity to explore the work of this distinguished designer. The charge was immeasureably enhanced by the survival of hundreds of photographs by Mattie Edwards Hewitt, Frances Benjamin Johnston, Jessie Tarbox Beals, and other photographers and material in the Rare and Manuscripts Collection, Carl A. Kroch Library, Cornell University, which forms the backbone of this research. Donated under the terms of Shipman's will, the collection consists of plans and drawings for several hundred projects representing most years of her practice, limited correspondence, and an exceptionally fine collection of photographs. The Cornell archive is uneven, however, and covers less than one half of Shipman's work. Material in other archives, transcripts of interviews with former employees, and magazine articles chronicling Shipman's peak years filled in some of the gaps. Shipman's Garden Note Book manuscript, loose-leaf notebooks, and lecture notes helped paint the larger picture with her own voice.

Reconstructing Shipman's life and career has been like working on a large, three-dimensional jigsaw puzzle, many pieces of which have been misplaced. Better documented than her own are the careers of her husband, playwright Louis Evan Shipman, and their son, Evan Biddle Shipman, a poet and journalist. The quest for details of Shipman's training and the founding of her practice was challenging, but as research progressed, my attention increasingly focused on her architectural design work that grew out of collaboration with many architects.

This book owes its inception to pioneering research by Daniel W. Krall, Associate Professor of Landscape Architecture, Cornell University, who dedicated many years to unraveling the career of Ellen Shipman. Krall's knowledge of her projects, working methods, and design intent is unsurpassed, and his generosity in sharing both his files and the frustration of the pursuit of Shipman is deeply appreciated. Others who provided critical information include Deborah Kay Meador, whose thesis work documents and assesses Shipman's Cornish years, and whose bibliography and client listing served as models for this book. Deborah Van Buren's dissertation and published writings on the Cornish colony and her interview with Shipman's longtime associate, Frances McCormic, have been invaluable. Noel Dorsey Vernon's interview with Eleanor Christie has been useful in understanding Shipman's office procedures. Ellen Biddle Shipman's grandchildren, Nancy Angell Streeter and Nicholas B. Angell, patiently answered my relentless queries about their grandmother's personal life and generously shared family mementoes.

Others who shared information, letters, or documents pertaining to Shipman include Noni Ames, Robin Bledsoe, Ann Bloom, Sarah Boasberg, Lucinda Brockway, Dona Caldwell, Richard Channick, Leslie Rose Close, Eleanor Cockfield, Christopher Combs, Hope Cushing, Reed Engle, Catherine Evans, Betsy Fitzsimmons, Mac Griswold, Mark Alan Hewitt, Martha Hill, Barbara Johnstone, Robin Karson, Richard Kenworthy, Diane McGuire, Margo Miller, William Noble, Jill Nooney, Patricia O'Donnell, Marion Pressley, Robin Reed, McDonald Sprague, Elizabeth Stone, David Streatfield, Maryanne Streeter, Patricia Thorpe, Eleanor Weller, and Lucy Ireland Weller.

Experts who generously contributed their specialized knowledge about Shipman's colleagues include Virginia Lopez Begg on Louisa Yeomans King, Robert Grese on Jens Jensen, Mark Alan Hewitt on Country Place Era architects, Robin Karson on Warren Manning and Fletcher Steele, Keith Morgan on Charles Platt, Sean O'Rourke on Evan Shipman, and Chris Vernon on Ossian Simonds. Those who actually went into the field to check remnants of commissions or who otherwise contributed to the client list include Richard Karberg (Cleveland), Joanne Lawson (Washington, D.C.), Helen Rollins (Maine), Janet Seagle (New Jersey), Joseph Tyree and Sally Gilmartin (Eastern Long Island), and Cynthia Zaitzevsky (Massachusetts).

Many people were helpful in my search for documents and resources or provided illustrations, including Charles Birnbaum, National Park Service Preservation Assistance Division; Suzy Berschbach, Grosse Pointe War Memorial; Virginia Colby, Cornish Historical Society; Lorna Condon, Society for the Preservation of New England Antiquities; William Louis Culberson, director, Sarah P. Duke Gardens; Jean Dodenhoff, Grosse Point Historical Society; John Dryfhout, curator, and Judith Nyhus, registrar, Saint-Gaudens National Historic Site, Department of Interior, National Park Service, Cornish, N.H.; Elaine Engst, curator of manuscripts, and her staff, Division of Rare and Manuscript Collections, Carl A. Kroch Library, Cornell University; Janet Evans, Pennsylvania Horticultural Society Library; Sherry Hollingsworth, Reynolda House; Michael A. Jehle, Nantucket Historical Association; Vicky Jones, manuscripts curator, Special Collections, University of Oregon; Jane Knowles, Schlesinger Library, Radcliffe College; Paul C. Lasewicz, archivist, Aetna; Paula McCloskey and Marcia Woodhams, Archives of American Gardens, Smithsonian Institution; Cheryl Mihalko, curator, University of Georgia; John Franklin Miller, former director, Stan Hywet Hall; Nancy Norwalk, Philip Read Memorial Library, Plainfield, New Hampshire; Chris Panos and Catha Grace Rambusch, Catalog of Landscape Records, Wave Hill, New York; Walter Punch, librarian, Massachusetts Horticultural Society Library; Lydia H. Schmalz, curator, Longue Vue Gardens; Carol Traynor, Society for the Preservation of Long Island Antiquities; Lt. Col. Rudy T. Veit, U.S. Military Academy, West Point; Donn Werling and Helen Hopkins, Fair Lane, Dearborn, Michigan; Hugh Wilburn, Frances Loeb Library, Harvard University; and Catherine Zusy, New Hampshire Historical Society.

During the short time available to complete this project, Robin Karson, executive director of the Library of American Landscape History, and publisher Ngaere Macray turned an awesome task into a pleasant endeavor. The book has been improved immensely by copyeditor Carol Betsch, assistance from Karen Krider and Joseph Tyree in compiling the bibliography, and invaluable suggestions from those who read drafts of the manuscript. David Broda's photoreproduction work has brought new life to illustrations of Shipman's projects.

INDEX

Page numbers in italics refer to illustrations.